ACCOLADES FOR

THE LOVE CYCLE OF A CICADA

"Stunningly beautiful. *The Love Cycle of a Cicada* is an intrepid story of patriotism and love for our time. Ken Ryan explores the meaning of commitment to country, family, and self across generations of people, technology—and cicadas—proving that heroism exists in many forms."

—Stuart George Ames—
Author of *The Sherpa's Burden: A Novel*

"Life's balance is often struggling to find a reason to survive when surrounded by loss. While following a road map is the safest path to a destination, what happens if you follow a missed connection? Peter's life is proof that tragedy and triumph can coexist and that sometimes in life, the heroes also need rescuing."

—Erin Dudley—
Journalist, *erinfdudley.com*

"Looking for an inspiring book about finding purpose, belonging, and redemption? Read *The Love Cycle of a Cicada* by Ken Ryan. Ken's story about an ambitious military man who fulfills a long ago promise to a childhood friend will leave you wondering how far you're willing to go to honor a commitment to someone who never left your heart."

—Jane Perdue—
Executive Director, The Jane Group
thejanegroup.org

The

Love
Cycle
of a
Cicada

Ken Ryan

United Writers Press
ASHEVILLE, N.C.

United Writers Press
Asheville, NC 28803
UWPnew.com

Copyright © 2024 by Ken Ryan

ISBN: 978-1-961813-61-8 (trade paperback)

ISBN: 978-1-961813-62-5 (ePub)

Cover art derived from photographs licensed via Pixabay and Shutterstock.com.

Printed in the USA

For all Gold Star families

"Hope is a constant force that pulls our lives
through the headwinds of time."
~ Ken Ryan ~

Acknowledgments

No author can live on a literary island and expect their work to ever see the light of day. I am indebted to numerous authors and editors for their advice, encouragement, and expertise that helped create this deeply personal, bucket-list achievement. For years, my writing coach and dear friend, Mary Johnston has provided a forum that allowed me to explore fiction as a vehicle to promote positive change for societal benefit. My fellow authors on this particular journey deserve a by-name shout out. They are Nicole Seitz, Stuart Ames, Richard Beck, Ann Combes, Erin Dudley, Tatiana and Trent Fasnacht, Jane Purdue, Lexi Stewart, Rob Turkewitz, and Thomas Ryan. I am indebted to Emily Furner for above and beyond line editing services, and to Vally Sharpe for orchestration of the final product. My family is everything, and without them, I am nothing. All love goes to my partner and best friend Kate, and my inspiring (military) children, Molly and Jeffrey.

And thank *you*…for taking the time to read *The Love Cycle of a Cicada*. May it inspire you to do something wonderful for those you love and for the community you live in.

The
Love
Cycle
of a
Cicada

CYCLE ONE

Triggers

Scientists use the term *trigger* to reference an event or object that causes a person to realize a memory in the present. People have some control over how frequently a memory is accessed. But the memory *trigger*? No control whatsoever.

1

1970
Beavercreek, Ohio
Early Spring

We lived a mere hour from Crosley Field—home of the Cincinnati Reds back then. My childhood revolved around baseball and the condition of the playground grass. Green signaled winter's end—time to take the glove out from under my pillow and remove the ball that molded the glove pocket.

Brown grass was practice grass. League play was over and it was time to fix what was broken, to think of new ways to get better. White snow was the signal to pack the gear and set goals for next season. If baseball was a calendar, the game was my wristwatch. The hands on the clock moved with each pitch, each at-bat, each third out and run to the dugout. On opening day in March 1970, baseball was ticking along nicely.

Like every other boy in Reds Nation, I had posters in my room of Johnny Bench, Cincinnati's catcher and future Hall of Famer. Mr. Bench could catch, of course. Fastballs, curves, screwballs. But he could also hit, and not just to get on base. He was known for knocking a few out of the park, and I dreamed of catching one of his home run balls whenever my dad and I visited Crosley Field for a few games each summer. "Mr. Bench is the leader on the field," Dad said as we watched him throw the ball back to the pitcher. "He motivates his teammates to do their best."

Those outings got me hooked on catching. I was determined to learn the craft and become the best backstop in Beavercreek. But catching equipment was too expensive for my dad's government salary from Wright-Patterson Air Force Base. So I made do with the shoddy equipment provided by our upstart baseball league. Each team had a catcher's bag that was handed down from season to season. It contained all the basics, except for a protective cup. The strings of the mitt and buckles on the chest protector needed constant repair. "All part of the game," the coaches would say as they struggled to secure the frayed straps on the shin guards between innings. They even mentioned that the Cincinnati Reds donated used equipment to the league. Perhaps my dodgy shin guards and stinky helmet were worn by the other Johnny—Johnny Edwards, the player traded for Mr. Bench. The coaches' tales got taller as the equipment aged and budgets tightened.

I didn't care. Catching made me feel cool. I was an eleven-year-old gearing up like a knight. My shin guards and chest protector were armor fortifying my inner gallantry and projecting my burgeoning courage. I donned the mask with pride. I commanded home plate, the geographic center of baseball activity and the epicenter for the game's respect. Playing catcher was the most important position in all of baseball, and the most fun, too.

At dinner on St. Patrick's Day, Dad announced that he had been offered a promotion. We were all excited until he said that to accept the job, we would have to move.

My metaphorical wristwatch stopped. Baseball season had just begun. As a catcher, I could control the placement of fielders with a shout, call a pitch with my finger, and let my dirty uniform speak for me as a leader. But I had no control over things like my dad asking and getting a job promotion—or their news that a little brother or sister was on the way.

I begrudgingly fell in line for our move east from Beavercreek, the first of many stressful uproots. Dad was assigned to an Air Force field office in northern Virginia. He started the new job right away, renting an apartment with a coworker and commuting back to Ohio on weekends. His noble intent was to keep me at Beavercreek Elementary School until summer, but Mom's morning sickness and general discomfort made it clear that we had to move sooner—smack dab in the middle of baseball season.

Mom broke the news during a round of backyard catch. "Your father found a nice house for us near a cute little school in a town called Woodland Hill. Daddy already checked out the school. The earlier we move, the quicker you can meet the neighborhood kids. You can make friends that will help you transition to junior high."

I tossed the ball to her, not knowing what to say.

"The best part of moving will be having your father home at night. He won't miss any of the fun that you and I are having. Are we having fun?" She threw the ball back.

I caught the ball and nodded, staring at the baseball's seams in my hand.

"We'll get our family time back, and Daddy will be able to help you with baseball again."

I did miss my dad and wanted father-son time back. But before I signed off on the move plan, I needed to claim something for myself.

"Can I paint my new bedroom red? Like the Cincinnati Reds?"

That provoked a tear and a hug. "Of course, you can!"

I should have driven a harder bargain and gotten some catcher's equipment out of the deal.

2

1970
Woodland Hill, Virginia
Late Spring

By April Fool's Day, we finished packing, and the movers drove the truck away. Less than twenty-four hours later, I was hanging up my Johnny Bench posters in my new bedroom. One or two adult couples stopped by to welcome us to the neighborhood, but since our new house was part of a recently constructed development, there were not many neighbors and no kids my age. I didn't know anyone when it came time to go to school.

On my first day at Woodland Hill, Miss Myers, my new teacher, introduced me by having me stand in front of the class. You would think nobody had ever heard of Ohio! I was unnerved and sought invisibility in my assigned seat in the last row near the window. I suppose her intent was to humanize me and disarm any gossip about who I was and how I got there. But I wish she had skipped the introduction. Now all the kids knew my name and I had no clue who they were or what their interests might be. I was mad at Miss Myers, but I forgave her quickly.

There were benefits of being placed in the corner of the last row.

Like a catcher, I had a vantage point from which to observe the players. I could choose who in the class to interact with…or melt away.

By Monday of the second week, I had all but decided to melt away. I tried to scope out the baseball players in the class and target them as potential friends with mutual interests. But Woodland Hill boys played soccer at recess. Even though I downplayed my struggle to make any friends so Mom wouldn't call the school or seek a meeting with Miss Myers, my woes were enough to guilt Dad into painting my bedroom Cincinnati red that Sunday. In between coats, Mom dropped some not-so-subtle advice on how to make friends.

"Go right up to someone and introduce yourself. Ask them if they want to play catch."

"They all play soccer."

"Well … join them."

"Or bring your baseball glove to school," Dad chimed in. Mom and I looked at him for elaboration. "If kids see you with your glove, they might ask you to play catch. It's a psychology trick for making a new friend." I didn't get the psychology part, but Mom's smile and nod made me think it was a good idea.

So, Monday of the third week, instead of melting away, I brought my baseball glove to school. "Dad's trick," as he called it, worked. Sort of. No one came up to me and asked to play catch at lunch, but a girl who played soccer with the boys at recess turned in my direction whenever Miss Myers had her back toward the class. Was she interested in me or my glove?

She looked at me. I kept my head down or looked out the window. When she faced forward, I snuck a glance at the back of her head. It was much more interesting than anyone else's in class. Her hair curled to the middle of her back like wet spaghetti, all twisted and curvy. It was dark red with golden brown streaks—somehow reminding me of the cinnamon doughnut I had had for breakfast. Sometime midweek, when she turned and stared at me, I found the courage to smile back. From that moment on, our glances danced between composition writing and multiplication drills.

The staring and smiling continued as we stood opposite each other during the geography bee. Miss Myers glanced at her index card and read my question. "Peter, on which continent is the country of Honduras located?"

"South America?"

"I'm sorry," she replied. "Please take your seat. The answer is North America."

I moped on my way back to the corner of the last row as the teacher announced with authority, "Next up is Lori."

"Ready, Miss Myers!" the girl declared.

Lori. I mumbled her name so I would remember. I had to stop calling her "Cinnamon" in my head. I would die if I ever called her that out loud.

Miss Myers responded in her best game-show host voice, "You are always ready. Here it comes."

The rest of the class laughed at the banter. I, however, grew anxious, hoping her question would be an easy one.

"On which continent does the Sinai Peninsula lie?" asked Miss Myers.

Lori's response was confident. "Africa."

"No, I'm sorry, Lori. The answer is Asia."

"No. It's not." Lori's combative response startled the room and the teacher.

Miss Myers paused. "Okay, Lori. Please explain yourself."

Lori was passionate. "Well Miss Myers, you taught us that the Sinai Peninsula belongs to the country of Israel because they won it in a war. But I looked it up with my mom. The peninsula was owned by Egypt before the war—so, since Egypt is in Africa and since war is the wrong way to fix a problem, Egypt should still own it, and therefore, the answer is Africa."

"Sit down, Lori."

"I'm right, aren't I, Miss Myers?"

"Please have a seat, Lori."

"Well? Am I right?"

Now annoyed, Miss Myers explained. "From a government ownership perspective, you may be right. However, this is a geography bee. The geography answer is Asia." She motioned for Lori to sit down.

Lori huffed but went to her seat as directed. She stole a glance at me and mouthed the words, "I know I'm right."

I didn't know the answer myself, but I nodded in agreement. She smiled and took her seat, looking satisfied that she had made her point.

Sometime between the geography bee and the end of the day, a note appeared in the web of my baseball glove. Wrapped in a tight triangle like a finger football, it had my name, Peter, written in an elegant script. Lori was my only suspect. I pushed the note deep into the pocket of my mitt so no one would see.

To get home, I took a small wooded path to my house, which was set in the middle of our half-built neighborhood. The entrance to the path was adjacent to the school's baseball field. I went to the backstop fence to read my mysterious correspondence alone, first looking around to see whether anyone was spying on me. I unfurled the triangle to read the note:

Are you going to the
skating party Friday night?

It was not signed.

Was the note from Lori, the geography bee girl with curly red hair? There was only one way to find out.

"MOM? THERE'S A SKATING PARTY at school on Friday night. Can I go?" I had just made spaghetti night much more interesting for my parents.

"Roller skating?"

"I guess so," I said. "I don't think the school is allowed to put ice on the gym floor." Dad laughed, and I laughed with him.

"Of course, you can go," Mom said. I could tell this fit her vision of meeting new kids and establishing a friend group. I didn't tell her about the note.

Dad brought up an issue I had failed to consider. "Do you know how to roller skate?"

Mom bailed me out. "He'll learn there, dear. It's a brave thing he's doing. Venturing into the unknown, trying a new activity." She turned to me in admiration. "We are very proud of you!"

To change the conversation topic, I asked something else that had been on my mind. "Hey, Dad? Do you think I could get my own catcher's mitt? Maybe one autographed by Johnny Bench?"

"For my son who's trying new things and setting a great example for the rest of the family, I think we can make that happen."

"Oh, and one more thing, Dad. I mean…if it's not too much trouble to ask." I was on a roll.

"What would that be, Peter?"

"Can I paint my room different from red?"

His puzzled face must have caught Mom's attention. "What color would you like it?"

"Is cinnamon a color?"

"You mean like a cinnamon doughnut?" asked Dad.

I'm sure I blushed as I nodded.

They looked at each other and Dad shrugged. "I'll buy the paint tomorrow on my way home from work," he said. "But you do the painting. Deal?"

"Deal," I replied.

Mom leaned over and whispered, "I'll help you. I like the color. I think it's a very creative idea."

I WANTED SO BADLY FOR Friday night to arrive, but in the meantime, I lived in a zone of blissful anticipation, my mind awash in a girl named Lori, who starred in my dreams as "Cinnamon."

On Thursday, she and I continued to eye-dance throughout the school day. That night, Mom had the wall opposite my bed prepped for painting. Dad came home early — with pizza — and we tackled the painting project as a family. As we sat on the floor against my bed, staring at the cinnamon-colored wall, Mom asked, "Do you like it?"

I was ecstatic but just nodded my approval and kept my mouth stuffed with pizza.

"I got something else at the store," said Dad. "Hang on. It's in the other room." I glanced at Mom, who shrugged.

He returned and presented me with a baseball bag full of new catcher's equipment, including a mitt autographed by Johnny Bench.

What a great day! This new house was turning out to be an okay place to live. I wished Thursday would never end but stopped myself, knowing that such a wish would prevent Friday from coming.

Thursday did end, and Friday began with Miss Myers providing a few nuggets of school history. Woodland Hill Elementary had a rich and proud tradition of roller-skating parties every month! That meant that everyone at school could skate. Mom and I discussed this fact in the car on the way to the party.

"You're an athlete, Peter. And a very good one! It might be hard at first, but remember, if you stick to it, you'll be good in no time."

"I'll fall down a lot."

"You're a catcher. You fall down all the time blocking pitches. Nothing ever gets by you. You always bounce back up like Johnny Bench and throw the runner out. So if you fall, get right back up. Be an example for your little brother." She kissed my head and pushed me out of the car. "Go have some fun and meet some friends."

I stood in line for skate rental, taking my cue from Miss Myers, who was directing the crowd. While a stream of confident skaters rolled into the gym, I sat, staring at my laced-up skates. I was in no hurry. When the hallway was empty, Miss Myers sent an encouraging look my way that helped me summon the nerve to stand. Bracing myself against the wall, I looked down at the rollers attached to my feet, which were already trying to point different directions. I stepped cautiously toward the gym. Once I was in, the blaring music drowned my panicked muttering. I stayed glued to the wall while the mob rolled counterclockwise around the floor. Not wanting to get sucked into the center, I developed a scheme to spend the rest of the night close to the walls.

I had no time to question why I had even bothered to attend this party. I was losing count of how many times I fell. Once at the corner farthest from the gym's exit, I fixated on returning to the safety of the hallway, which motivated me to roll a greater distance without falling. Looking up and ahead instead of at my feet had a very positive effect. My confidence soared, but a bump and a spill just short of the hallway entrance soured the moment. I decided I either should not have attended or should have worn my new catcher shin guards so at least my knees would have been spared the pain of my one and only lap around the gym.

I crawled to a spot in the hallway where no one from the gym, including Miss Myers, could see me. I plotted how I could stay there unnoticed until the party was over. Just as I decided to take off my skates, Cinnamon rolled up. "Hey, Peter. What's the matter? You tired or something?"

"I'm tired of falling down."

She laughed, though I didn't intend to be humorous.

"Let me show you how not to fall down." She reached out and said, "You just gotta hold my hand and not let go."

I grasped her hand and did not let go. Not for the whole rest of the party. Except for the hokey pokey. I almost fell as we turned ourselves around, but she grabbed my arm, and everything was right again.

When the gym teacher blew the whistle and the music stopped, we skated together to the hallway where Miss Myers was overseeing the skate removal and return. Cinnamon helped me to a spot and said, "You can let go now."

I didn't want to, but I had to get the blasted skates off my feet. She sat, and I fell down next to her. "Thanks for helping me learn to skate."

"Did you have fun? I hope you did. It's no fun falling at a skating party. I think you learned quick. Oh, here comes Miss Myers. Watch her face." She yelled, "Miss Myers. Do you want to smell my feet?"

Our sixth-grade teacher cringed at the thought. "No thank you, Lori. I get enough of that smell when you and the boys come in from recess." We both laughed.

Lori. Her name is Lori. *Not* Cinnamon. I fixated on calling her by her proper name, but I wasn't good at holding a conversation. Grasping for something to say, I remembered recess. "Is soccer your favorite sport?"

She laced her sneakers. "I like other sports better, but I'm not allowed to bring my hockey stick to school. I play soccer with the boys because they let me."

"Do you play hockey? I guess that's why you're a good skater."

"I play field hockey. It's played on grass instead of ice. My sister, Patty, is in high school, and she's teaching me how to play since there are no leagues for sixth graders to join." She paused. "I liked your baseball glove. How come you brought it to school?"

"I thought someone who plays baseball would want to play catch. Baseball is my favorite sport."

She stood and helped me up, offering me the pleasure of holding her hand once again. "I like baseball," she said, "but not as much as hockey. That doesn't mean we can't play together."

We walked toward the school's exit.

"I have an idea," she said. "Why don't we meet tomorrow at the baseball field for modified catch?"

"What do you mean by modified?"

Lori brushed back her wavy hair and continued. "Well, I like to practice field hockey against the backstop at the baseball field, but it's hard to do by myself, and Patty has been too busy to play with me. I could hit my shots at you, and you could catch the ball with your baseball glove. We'd be combining two sports into one. I practice hockey, and you practice baseball. What do you think?"

I was excited and borrowed a phrase from Mom. "It's a very creative idea." I added, "My dad just bought me a new catcher's mitt. This will help me break it in."

"You better bring all your catcher's gear. I can hit the ball pretty hard."

Mom's car was waiting for me at the school roundabout. "Do you have a ride? My mom can take you home if you need one."

"I'm okay. But thanks anyway. My brother Michael is coming to pick me up. He's not here yet, but I'm sure he's on his way."

"Okay." I started to walk away, but a chivalrous feeling overcame me. "I'll wait here with you until he comes." It was twilight, so I couldn't see if she blushed, but I was almost positive a dimple appeared on her left cheek. I needed to make the conversation less mushy, so I asked her what the secret to skating was, and she filled me in on her technique and the confidence-building methods that made her such an expert.

"My big brother Michael taught me how to skate. He said the secret is not to let go of the friend who is teaching you. Holding on to someone gives you confidence. I think it worked in my case. And now that I taught you, you can teach someone else."

"My little brother," I said. "Except he's not born yet. I'll have to wait a few years to teach him."

"Well then, you and I will have to practice some more so you can be a good teacher." Lori lowered her head. "I can't skate with Michael anymore. He's joining the Army."

"Oh." I had no better response.

Her eyes wandered. "He told us last night. My dad didn't take it well. My mom cried." She paused. "Michael graduates from high school next month. Then he said he has to go to Louisiana. He told me joining the Army is what he wants to do."

Before my silence became too awkward—and my ignorance too obvious—her brother's car appeared, and her smile returned. She took my hand one last time. "Always remember the secret to skating. 'Don't let go.'" I looked at her hand and up to her dimple. She ran to catch her ride, shouting, "See you tomorrow! Ten o'clock."

I watched her cinnamon hair bounce into the twilight.

I HAD TO BREAK THE news to my dad that our father-son time on Saturday morning would have to be postponed. He was a little disappointed, but Mom understood. I think she was watching Lori and me from the car while sitting in the roundabout. I wanted to walk to school but because I had all my catcher's gear stuffed into a baseball bag, she offered to drive me.

Instead of arriving by car, Lori emerged from the woods. I was elated. She lived in the neighborhood next to mine and within walking distance of my house!

I put on my new catcher's gear, mask, and all. She went to the flat spot of dirt just shy of the pitcher's rubber. "I usually shoot from here. You can tell because the grass is all worn down."

"Can I show you my new glove?" She nodded and we met halfway between her spot and home plate. I spread my mitt, turning it front and back for her. "It's clean now. We need to get it dirty. And the best way to break it in is to pound it with lots of catches."

"Oh, I think I can do that." She showed me the field hockey ball she used. "Will this do? I think it's about the same size as a baseball."

She flipped me the ball, and I went back to home plate. "I'll test it with a throw to second base. I'll pretend there's a guy stealing." Though I wanted to make sure I could maneuver with all my new equipment on, my real motivation was to show off my arm. I squatted as if receiving a pitch and then sprang up and threw a perfect strike to second base, catching the imaginary stealer for the third out.

"Nice throw," she said, with a smile, "too bad our second baseman was pretend."

"I'll get it," I said, embarrassed. I ran out to centerfield, got the ball, and returned it to her. "The field hockey ball is a little heavier than a baseball. But it's close enough. Batter up!" She nodded, and we went to our positions to have a baseball-hockey catch session.

As I crouched in a catcher's squat, something didn't feel right. I'd forgotten my cup. Dad's rule for the cup was to always wear it at official baseball games and practices. I rationalized that the rule did not apply today — we were just having fun, right? I regretted my lapse in judgment after Lori wound up for her first swing. The speed of the ball off her stick surprised me. The ball bounced once on its way to home plate and then over my glove, straight into my groin. Instantly, I understood why fathers make some rules for their sons. I tried to maintain my squat — and avoid embarrassment — but finally fell forward and curled up in pain. Lori came and knelt by my side while I writhed in the dirt at home plate.

"I'm all right," I whimpered. My catcher's mask hid the tears welling up in my eyes.

"Maybe there's a hole in your new glove, Peter," she said with a hint of laughter. "Just breathe normal. The pain will go away in a few minutes. This happens to my brother all the time. He's a catcher, just like you." After a quiet pause, she changed the subject. "Do you know where Vietnam is?"

"Not really," I grunted.

"That's where Michael is going after he finishes training in Louisiana. He told me last night in the car." She drew a heart in the dirt with her foot. "My daddy is very angry. My parents were yelling at each other last night. I didn't get much sleep."

I sat back on my butt, taking a few deep breaths as the pain subsided, still listening while she continued staring at the ground. "I don't like yelling," she said. "I like it here. The way it is now. Quiet. Peaceful." She looked at me, straining to see my eyes through the catcher's mask. "You okay now?"

"Yeah. I'll do better next time. I really am a good catcher."

"I know you are," she said, smiling. "But let's just stay here one more minute." I appreciated the extra time to recover.

She surprised me with her next question.

"Peter, is your little brother a mistake?"

"What do you mean? I don't think so."

"Well, Daddy said I was a mistake. I heard him say that to Mom last night."

I took off my mask and finger-combed my hair back in place while she drew in the dirt. She glanced toward the woods. "Listen. Do you hear them?"

I concentrated on where she was looking and heard a hollow sound. "I think I do."

"It's the cicadas."

"What are cicadas?"

"They're bugs that live in the ground. My mom says that when they're ready, they come out of the ground all at once."

"Ready for what?"

"To mate!"

I wasn't sure what she meant at the time. I think she sensed my unease, so she sidestepped an explanation. "I've been hearing them, and there are a bunch of their shells on the trees in the woods. But I don't see any flying. I bet they're still high in the trees drying their wings. Mom says cicadas are like caterpillars who turn into butterflies, but they are much uglier."

She gave me a side glance. "Are you okay to play?"

"I am. I just wasn't expecting the ball to come at me so fast. You are a great hockey player."

"I'm the best! But there's no hockey team to join for a few years, so I guess you're one of the few who knows." She offered her hand to lift me off the ground, like she had the night before.

Now that I was recovered, our game of hybrid-catch proceeded without interruption. I grew comfortable catching her slap shots, and my glove was getting a great workout. But the noise from the woods grew louder and louder until I could barely hear Lori's hockey stick connect with the ball.

She looked up toward the sky. "I think we need to stop." Her eyes traced the movement of bugs that were starting to appear all around us. "Quick! Pack your stuff. We need to go to the outfield to see this."

"See what?"

"The cicadas. Today is emergence day. Let's go watch them fly!"

I packed up and slung the baseball bag over my shoulder, waiting for her next instruction. She grabbed my hand, and we ran through left field and up the ridge to the school's tree-lined boundary, but I had trouble keeping up.

"Drop the bag, Peter. We'll get it later." I did as instructed, trusting that this was some sort of adventure and not a trick.

We stopped in the far corner of the school property, next to the woods that separated the school from surrounding housing developments. Against the wooded backdrop, insects flew everywhere and all around us.

Lori beamed. "My mom told me this was going to happen! She said she saw them when my sister was born. They're the Brood X cicadas. They come out every seventeen years." She let go of my hand, stepped into the swarm, and spun around, her hair flying out—each wavy strand extending to its farthest outward reach. She stopped and raised her eyes, following the cicadas, that dimple accentuating her smile.

I stood like I was on roller skates again, unsure of my emotional footing. A bug landed on my shoulder, and I shouted in alarm. I ducked, squirmed, and worked my way back toward her, looking for guidance on how to handle the strangeness that surrounded us.

Lori, in all her happiness, met me and plucked the cicada off my shoulder. "Relax, Peter. This guy's not going to hurt you." She placed the bug in her other hand. It looked big in her palm, but only because its wings were quite long compared to its body. "Look at his eyes. Don't they look goofy?" She was referring to the cicada's bulbous red protrusions.

"They live underground for seventeen years," she explained, raising her voice to overpower the cackling noises surrounding us. "And when they need to find a mate, they all come out at the same time." There was that word again.

Lori stood really close to me, but she had turned away, eyes focused on the tornado of bugs. Once again, I stared at the back of her head, but this time up close and more admiringly. That was before two cicadas landed on her hair.

"Cinnamon!" I shouted at the bugs to leave and reached out to shoo them away. Lori turned in my direction, causing my hands to shoot through her hair, where they locked on the back side of her head. Her arms slipped around my waist, and there we were—lips meeting in one of the most secluded spaces on earth.

JASON, MY NEW LITTLE BROTHER, made his appearance over the summer. As a result, when I wasn't outside with my catcher's mitt, I spent a lot of time in my room reading, playing tabletop baseball with a pair of dice, and listening to popular music on the radio. Mom's favorite singer, Neil Young, had just released a song that mentioned Ohio.

My dad explained to me later what happened at Kent State University. It made me sad, and I told him about Lori's brother going to Vietnam. He assured me everything would be all right—he even went to meet Lori's family to see if they needed anything. That made me feel better.

One afternoon, I rummaged through my closet and found an activity stamp book entitled *Wonders of the Animal Kingdom*, one of many obsessive-compulsive indulgences that had occupied me in my early elementary school years. As I flipped through the book, I came upon sticker number 364 in the insect section—the cicada. The drawing reminded me of that spring day when I played my first round of catch with Lori. In the blank space next to the stamp, I wrote a poem—beginning a penchant for uniting life and words.

A girl at school put a note in my glove.
A new best friend? A first true love?
Is she someone to share my hopes, dreams, and fears?
Is she a friend for a day, a month, or years?

CYCLE TWO

Gouge

Gouge is Navy jargon for the advice a sailor needs to thrive in a new assignment. Seamen and airmen are not afforded much time to digest the how and why of warfighting. That is when gouge comes in—it's team building, sailor-to-sailor talk that covers the knowledge gaps.

3

1987
Indian Ocean
Late Winter

Three-quarters of a mile isn't a lot of ocean, especially when you have to land a helicopter at the end of it. I was deployed on the aircraft carrier USS Kitty Hawk, steering my SH-3H Sea King helicopter behind the carrier, intercepting the final-approach glideslope. Shifting my eyes from the instrument panel to the ship's optical landing aid provided relief from a leaning sensation of vertigo. I caught the guiding beam of light as it pierced the darkness, drawing me like a moth to the pitching and rocking flight deck. I took a deep breath before toggling the radio on the cyclic control stick. "Sea King Ball," I radioed, signifying the handoff from approach control to the landing signals officer, Paddles.

Paddles broadcast in an upbeat, confident tone. "Roger, Ball." Rough seas and overcast skies were making the air-wing recovery cycle difficult this evening, but Paddles had coaxed them all down safely. We were his last plane for the night.

"You good?" Mongo, my copilot, asked over the intercom.

"I'm good," I replied, even though I was white knuckling the stick a bit more than usual. Chief Parks and Petty Officer Bondurant sat at their mission consoles in the aft station. I sensed their concern as Paddles used more words than usual to coach our helicopter down the glideslope.

"You're a little bit high, Sea King. Ship's pitching...ease her down. There you go. Watch your power..."

As I flew the aircraft over the deck edge, seventy feet above the waves, the air boss in the control tower took verbal command from Paddles and directed me to my landing spot.

"Sea King, you are cleared to spot four."

Red and green flashlight wands from a line division signalman guided me to the bright white landing circle. Once on deck, Mongo signaled the maintenance crew to chock and chain the helicopter while the rotors continued to spin. Mongo, Parks, Bondo, and I stayed glued to our shutdown tasks until the engines were silenced and the rotating blades braked. I breathed a sigh of relief.

Still connected to the intercom, Mongo checked my mental pulse. "Vertigo get you on final, PB?"

"Passed Ball"—or PB for short—was my squadron call sign, an annoying reminder of the one play that ended my promising baseball career and signaled a turn to naval aviation. I'm so used to being called PB that I forget my real name until I read a letter from home.

"A little bit," I responded and then offered an alibi for the whole crew to hear. "We've had so many uneventful flights together. I just wanted to shake things up a bit for the crew."

"That you did, sir," chimed Chief Parks. "But Bondo here is on his third flight today. Nothing you did was going to wake him up."

"I was awake the whole time," Bondo protested.

Mongo refocused us. "Since you did all the work landing this piece of metal, I'll take care of the post-flight engine wash."

"You got it, Mongo. See you downstairs." I disconnected my intercom cord, unstrapped myself from my seat harness, and stepped gingerly over the lower center console to get to the port side door. I dropped the door down so that it became a stairwell. As I descended, I soaked in the industrial ambiance of the flight deck. It was familiar and comforting to me, a naval aviator in the prime of my flying years. I had over one thousand flight hours in my three-year tour. As the most senior lieutenant in the squadron, I was a steward to a cause bigger than myself.

A baseball career would have been fun, but a pilot's life parallels the national pastime in many ways. I geared up like a catcher for each flight, donning over fifty pounds of survival gear and safety equipment. Every mission was a ballgame, and every task within that mission was an inning. Commanding a crew, optimizing every task, and landing safely was gratifying and always left me yearning for the next flight.

I also loved the physicality of flying. A helicopter was, after all, heavy equipment. Being assigned to chase submarines while using a mix of technology—sonar, sonobuoys, and a magnetic anomaly detector—was a multi-task dream. The squadron was my team, and I was proud of the mission and my part in its accomplishment. I had a purpose and gave the job my total commitment.

As helicopter exhaust fumes dissipated and the equatorial Indian Ocean air enveloped the flight deck, I turned my attention to the sailors working in and around the air-wing jets that had just landed. We were on our seventy-fifth straight day at sea but each day required us to perform at our best while compartmentalizing our anxieties. Channel fever — when thoughts of beer and a few days away from the grind compete for a sailor's focus — is an occasional malady remedied by a port call. Homesickness, however, is a chronic condition requiring therapeutics best addressed in the privacy of a bunk. Only as a team did we get through the cruise without losing our minds.

Still helmeted, I exited the Sea King, walking from the nose to the tail rotor along the starboard side. I inspected every inch of the helicopter using my flashlight beam to find evidence of hydraulic or oil leaks. Seeing none, I turned toward the ship's superstructure — the island — that housed the air boss's control tower and the captain's bridge. A team of flight deck handlers was unloading the COD, the carrier onboard-delivery airplane, that had just landed. Her cargo offload contained supplies, spare parts, and mail for the crew. I loved getting mail, but my fingers were crossed for a gyroscope we needed to return a problematic helicopter to flight-capable status. I was the squadron quality assurance officer. My division was responsible for aircraft safety, and I was the primary maintenance-check flight pilot.

I met Chief Parks and Bondo outside the rotor arc and pointed to the COD. Parks smiled and yelled over the low-power jet engine whines all around us. "Mail call for sure!"

"I'd rather get a port call," Bondo replied.

"I'll take a gyro," was my nerdy retort. But it was the truth. They chuckled as we found our way through the night to the catwalk.

At the base of the catwalk stairwell stood my quality assurance chief petty officer, who gave me a thumbs up. I read his mustached lips, "The gyro! We got it!"

Over the sound of crashing waves on the ship's bow seventy feet below, I yelled back to him. "Great! Have night-check install the gyro. Get the bird to the flight deck. I'll get the maintenance officer to authorize an engine turn in the morning and follow through with operations to get an afternoon check flight. If she stays in the hangar any longer, she'll be cannibalized for parts."

He patted me on the shoulder. "Fixing the hanger queen is my top priority. It will be your going away present!" I totally missed the going away part.

I continued along the dark catwalk toward the maintenance-control space for post-flight paperwork. As my eyes adjusted to the darkness of the catwalk, I heard a voice barking orders and water came at me from six junior night-check maintenance workers, their faces filled with glee at the opportunity to douse an officer. My helmet, visor, and survival gear took most of the surge, but at least one bucket—the coldest, I'm convinced—found my neck and upper torso.

The first to shake my hand was Airman Gott. "Congratulations on your last flight, sir. We are going to miss you."

I embraced the moment and shook every hand in front of me but was confused. I addressed the maintenance officer who'd commanded the bucket brigade, "What's going on, MO?"

"A wetting down for your last flight. Navy tradition."

"But it's not my last flight. I need to fly a maintenance-check tomorrow. The gyro arrived."

"Mongo will fly it. Skipper wants your ass in the ready room ASAP. I'll let him explain. Chief Parks can cover your post-flight paperwork."

"I'll take your gear, sir," Gott said with a grin. I handed him a soggy pile in exchange for a towel.

I paused at the hatchway and removed my boots. I didn't want to keep the commanding officer waiting, but I also did not want to scuff up the spit-shine floors with soggy boots out of respect for the hard-working sailors who swabbed these decks every night. It took me about ten seconds to shuffle in my socks across the tiled floor to the ready room—time enough for my mind to wander to my first flight in the squadron nearly three years before—a man-overboard launch in the middle of a moonless night.

It was my third day in the squadron. I arrived aboard ship by COD alongside the prospective executive officer, Commander Russ Rasmussen. "Razz" was an icon in the Navy helicopter community, a Silver Star recipient for a combat rescue in the Vietnam War.

I had been assigned as an alert-crew copilot. Even though I was a new check-in, I was trained and ready for the assignment, or so I thought. I was paired with a braggart lieutenant commander who was twice passed over for promotion and carried a chip on his shoulder. He enjoyed abusing his junior copilots and I had run into a stressful flight environment without proper indoctrination. I found this out after we crashed.

"MAN OVERBOARD," bellowed the bridge watch on the ship's internal communication system. Those words put me into a sprint from my stateroom rack to the ready room, where crews assemble for last-minute situational updates. I was told to meet my pilot at the aircraft on the flight deck.

I strapped in my seat and buried my head in the pocket checklist, furiously trying to accomplish my copilot tasks by flashlight. The hover-altitude knob was set at zero to comply with an earlier routine-maintenance procedure. I was too new and inexperienced to realize that he had already flown us into a low hover before I could set the proper altitude on the automatic flight control system.

The pilot — without my concurrence — engaged the automatic system himself and the aircraft flew to the exact altitude it was told to. Zero feet. A wave hit the rotor blades. We flipped left-side down and everything went dark. The crew and pilot managed to get out right away and swim to the surface, escaping through up-facing windows and doors. I, however, was trapped in the sinking vessel.

I tried without success to open the left escape window as water poured in from the now-empty pilot side. Thankfully, an air pocket had formed aft in the crew cabin. I swam to it, took one deep breath, and crawled my way — underwater — out the crew's door. The "man overboard" was later identified as a strobe light on a fishing buoy bobbing in the waves.

I appreciated the irony—I'd gotten wet on my first flight in the squadron—and on my final one.

"Attention on deck!" yelled the duty officer as I opened the ready room door. I dropped my boots and locked myself to attention. Eyes forward, I scanned for the only two officers afforded this protocol— the air-wing commander or the battle group admiral.

"Get in here, Passed Ball. We're doing this for you."

There was no mistaking Razz's pitched voice. He had stood by me throughout the crash investigation and subsequent appearance before the Field Naval Aviator Evaluation Board, mentoring me through the process. Without his support, my first flight in the squadron might also have been my last. Razz was a great guy—throughout his tenure as the executive officer, and then in command, he replaced a toxic squadron climate with a professional focus on mission accomplishment.

Squadron pilots packed the ready room. I went to Razz's side and faced my peers in my stocking feet. He barked an order to Commander Kendall, the executive officer. Kendall's call sign was K-dog, but in a group setting, referring to him as XO was the proper protocol.

"XO, read the good news from Washington, D.C."

"Aye, aye, Skipper." K-dog read the official notice with embellishment.

"FROM THE DEPARTMENT OF THE NAVY, NAVAL AIR TEST CENTER, PATUXENT RIVER, MARYLAND. TO LIEUTENANT PASSED BALL KNUCKLEHEAD. CONGRATULATIONS ON YOUR SELECTION TO ATTEND THE U.S. NAVAL TEST PILOT SCHOOL AS A MEMBER OF CLASS..."

He handed me the paper copy for me to read the rest. "It happened, PB. The primary knucklehead dropped out. They want you at Pax River. You're going to be a test pilot!"

I was shocked, embarrassed, humbled, and confused—all at the same time. Even though I had been selected as an alternate for the highly competitive helicopter pilot slot at the Naval Test Pilot School, I was realistically planning to transfer to the shore-based SH-3H fleet-replacement training squadron when the cruise was over. But as the wardroom erupted in applause, it sunk in. I made it. I squatted catcher style, hanging my head low to hide tears of joy.

Razz reached down to lift me up. "The timeline is short, PB. We are going to get you on a COD to Diego Garcia in two days so you can get home to San Diego and square away your personal affairs. The XO is setting up a farewell dinner for you tomorrow in the officer's mess."

He paused, fighting his own emotions. "We are going to miss you. But on behalf of the entire command, congratulations. I know you will do well at test pilot school and meet all the challenges that come afterward in your follow-on tours. You know, this may also be your ticket to the astronaut program. We are proud of you." He gave me a bro-hug, and the room erupted in another round of applause.

I shook hands with all my squadron mates, except for Mark, my roommate and best friend, who was standing watch duty in the Battle Group Commander spaces. His squadron call sign was "Trashman." He was our intelligence officer.

Soaked as I was, I hustled to my stateroom, thinking I would write to my parents and my brother Jason. As I looked for paper, it dawned on me that no written letter by mail would beat a phone call from the island of Diego Garcia, so instead, I changed into dry skivvies and a fresh flight suit.

I was careful to first remove a keepsake that I kept in my shoulder pocket — a POW/MIA bracelet. I put the bracelet back in my dry flight suit, then pumped my fist and yelled, "Yes!"

Before I could dwell on the sudden change in my future career plans, Trashman burst through the door. "I heard a rumor my roommate is going to be an astronaut!"

I grinned. "One step at a time. Test pilot first."

"Details, details." We embraced and then just stared at each other.

"I'm leaving in two days," I said.

"Good. I've always wanted a stateroom to myself. Besides, we're all leaving in a few weeks. This cruise can't last forever. I'll miss you, but heck, we're friends. Good friends always find a way to stay in touch."

"For sure."

Trash pulled some mail from the watch logbook he carried. "I'm on break right now. I intercepted the admin petty officer in the passageway and got our mail. These letters are yours. The usual five from your mom." He dumped a stack onto my desk and then held a pink envelope up to his nose. "But this one is, well, let's just say it doesn't smell like a letter from your mom."

I grabbed it from him. "It's from Lori. My old friend from junior high. You know the story. Cruise pen-pals since we left port in the Philippines. Nothing serious. More like a whim."

He raised an eyebrow and grinned. "Sometimes all it takes is a whim. I married my whim."

"And I'm glad you did. I'll miss ravaging through Mrs. Trashman's care packages."

Trash looked at his watch. "I can be a few minutes late. You haven't told me much about Lori. I want to know more. Is this the start of a serious relationship? Who's leading, and who's following?"

"Okay, here's the gouge. I don't know if it's serious. The letters are casual. Some minor flirting. We were best friends all through junior high until I moved back to Ohio for high school. Lori played field hockey, so I would be her goalie in my catcher gear to help her practice her shots. She also threw a mean fastball, so she pitched batting practice for me."

"Junior high is hard for everyone," I sighed. "But her family was dealing with heavier issues. Her brother Michael was in the Army serving in Vietnam, and he went missing."

Trash leaned back against the stateroom lockers. "Heavier is an understatement."

"I understand more now the trauma her family was going through, but back then, I was just an immature jock. She was in trouble, and I didn't give her the support she needed. We were in two different places emotionally when I moved away. Now…" I paused. Words escaped me.

Trash filled in the blank space. "Now you might be in the same place. Emotionally speaking, I mean."

I shrugged and smiled. "She reached out to me, and I'm thrilled. But I can tell that Michael's disappearance still haunts her. In one of her letters, she updated me that the Army still lists him as missing. I try to imagine what it would be like not knowing where my brother was for fifteen years. Our Navy survival training brought home that point. Remember SERE school?"

Trash sat down at his desk. "Survival, evasion, resistance, and escape. Does one ever forget being waterboarded?"

"I thought about Lori's brother the whole time I was getting slammed against the wall by a Navy SEAL. Did Michael evade? Was he imprisoned? Could he still be alive? Is he being beaten at this moment?" I pulled the POW/MIA bracelet from my flight suit shoulder pocket. It was inscribed with Michael's full name. "I don't wear this on my wrist anymore, uniform regs and all. But I keep it in my flight suit, a lucky charm of sorts. My mom donated in Michael's honor and gave me the bracelet to help me understand what was going on with Lori's family.

I handed the bracelet to Trash, who examined its inscription. "I've never told Lori about it," I said.

"You should tell her, PB. These bracelets may be popping up again sometime soon. I'm reading reports of a seismic shift occurring in the Soviet Union. Mother Russia may be losing grip of her satellite countries and the impact could be drastic. When you finish reading your letters, come on down to the battle watch. I'll show you the top-secret intelligence feeds. You can see for yourself what I'm talking about." He handed the bracelet back. "In the meantime, I'll leave you two alone." Trash sniffed the letter once more. "The words may say one thing, but the fragrance is sending a definite message. Make sure you leave room in your busy test pilot future for a whim." He dropped it on my desk and left.

I didn't open the letter right away. I just held it, smelled it, and soaked in its potential meaning. My quiet moment ended with the noise of a steam catapult, designed to fling a thirty-ton aircraft off the ship and into the air at one-hundred-and-fifty miles per hour. The nightly catapult checks were starting, and they were doing their best to destroy my eardrums.

I pulled my Sony Walkman from my desk drawer, donned the headphones, pressed PLAY, and rolled the volume to LOUD. If my hearing was going to get destroyed, I preferred it be by The Cure.

Then I opened the envelope.

Dear Peter,

Forgive me for not using your squadron call sign – Passed Ball. You always caught everything I hit at you...though not always with your glove! I hope this letter reaches you on a day when you aren't too busy and have time to relax. (My bet is that those times are rare. I remember from junior high that you never sat still, an admirable trait in my book!) Most of all, I hope this letter finds you safe and happy.

For my own peace of mind, I want you to be safe. But I understand that flying helicopters – on a ship in the middle of the ocean, no less – makes you happy. It's what you love to do. And I get that it's what our country wants you to do. (Michael said the same thing before he left for the Army.) So, it's a win-win, huh?

A smiley face was hand-drawn in the right margin.

In your last letter, you mentioned that after deployment, you will settle in San Diego for your next assignment. (If I haven't told you, I love getting your letters! I feel so close to you as I read them. Keep them coming!) It stinks that you were selected as an alternate for test pilot school. I hope the Navy wakes up one day and realizes their mistake. I know how much you want to be an astronaut and that test piloting is how you can get there! That is just so cool...but so is everything else you've done in your career. Your parents are very proud of you. (Hint: I called your mom again.) So am I!

Thank you for asking about Michael. It pains me to think about what he is going through. I am just now starting to emerge from the shadow of his disappearance. That dark day in March of

'72 is seared in my mind. I was shooting baskets in the driveway when the Army officer and our pastor pulled up. I yelled for my mom, but my dad burst through the door. He must have known why they were there. Patty and Mom soon followed.

Daddy fell to his knees in the mud that was our front yard. Seeing him, we all figured it out. Michael was gone. Mom ran back into the house. I attempted to go to Daddy, but Patty stopped me and took me inside. We cried while the men consoled our dad.

Their conversation came through the door. "Missing, not dead." Those are the only words I heard that mattered. "Missing, not dead." They changed the descriptor over the years: "missing in action," "unaccounted for," "not yet recovered." But "missing, not dead" is the curse that destroyed my family.

Patty is leading our family effort to find Michael. She's organizing a petition to Congress and the Defense Department to find out more about any search efforts. I took a political science class at the community college to learn about countries in that region, hoping to help my sister. Relations with Vietnam are strained, but Patty is persistent.

The ship's ten o'clock broadcast interrupted my reading. "Tattoo, Tattoo, lights out in five minutes. Stand by for evening prayer." As the chaplain read a prayer, I continued with the letter.

When Michael disappeared, my family fell apart. We have not heard from Mom in years. Patty continues to take care of Daddy and all of his medical appointments. I have been bouncing around northern Virginia earning money to pay for classes at the community college. Patty said she will make sure I get your letters until I get settled somewhere. She's helped see me through all my pain and confusion. I need some of your purpose and passion.

Peter, I tell you this because I feel I can. We were buddies on the ballfield. Now you are my sailor so far away at sea. I miss you, and I miss Michael. I miss having my family together. I know I have to take many steps to fix myself and my attitude. I am not a mistake, and I should stop feeling like one. Thank you for never making me feel that way!

I love you, Peter. There, I said it. I am going to seal this letter and send it before I lose my courage.

Be safe!! Maybe I can be the girl you dream about on your tough days. If we can't be together, I'd settle for that. I can be your motivation to do the right thing and make the right choices. Michael told me in his last letter from Vietnam that I was his girl. He said he thought of me when he was having a hard time and needed inspiration.

But Michael didn't come back. I always want you to come back.

Love, Lori

I stared at my cluttered fold-down desk. In truth, I was searching for a response to Lori's declaration of love, newly in the context of receiving my dream assignment as a test pilot.

A piece of paper slid under my door. It was the next day's flight schedule. As the ship turned, gravity rolled my chair to the door, where I scooped up the schedule. My name was not on any of the twelve flight sorties, nor did I have any training or administrative meetings to attend. I sighed. They'd benched me.

The fragrance of Lori's letter remained in the air. I would respond tonight, but not now — my pen was missing, my socks were wet, and I was hungry. And there was still a matter of visiting Trashman in the battle watch spaces.

I donned new socks and laced up my still-damp flight boots. I placed the letter in my front pocket, close to my heart. Returning Michael's bracelet to its place in my left shoulder pocket, I stepped out the door to visit my roommate.

I paused just outside the stateroom. The infinite mirror effect in the empty passageway created by ten identical watertight doorframes was one of my favorite parts of the ship. I walked through each hatch, adjusting my gait to avoid the knee-knockers until I reached the shiny, blue-tiled section. I took a sharp right to face a smoked-glass security window. There, I presented my identification card through a slot and was buzzed in by the attendant. I thought of offering a confession to the smoky window but doubted there was a Catholic behind the glass who would get the joke.

The battle watch foyer was abuzz with desk activity. Sailors and officers scoured through reams of paper that poured out of dozens of dot-matrix printing machines. They were the admiral's copy editors for intelligence — the cutters-and-pasters of the big picture. The admiral's worldview wholly depended on their thoroughness.

I seldom troubled myself with big-picture intelligence. Through training, banter, and catwalk chitchat, Trashman told me everything I needed to know. Helicopter parts, performance, and personnel were my specialties. Later in my career, if I served long enough, the big picture would matter — but not now.

From the foyer, I parted a curtain and stepped into a darkened, blue-lit array of panels, scopes, and consoles — some the size of a baby grand piano. The library-like quiet was occasionally interrupted by radio chatter from bridge-to-bridge communication piped through loudspeakers. Vessels exchanged details about course and speed as they maneuvered in the night formation. The big screen displayed a projection of the water space out to one thousand miles, and it sat smack in front of the room's biggest seat — the battle group admiral's chair. Call sign "Alpha Bravo." The projector glare reflected off the balding head of its occupant, giving away a mustachioed imposter — my buddy, Trashman.

I approached with reverence, being careful not to disrupt the focused professional atmosphere, and whispered, "Admiral Trash, I presume?"

Not a flinch from the screen. "You can call me Alpha Bravo, for I am the Battle Watch." He turned to me and bounced his eyebrows, Groucho Marx style.

"And a pompous one at that."

"I resemble that remark."

I rolled my eyes at the classic Marxism, and he continued. "Besides, I own this chair while the admiral is in the rack. At least until the real battle watch captain comes back from mid-rats." He referred to the midnight rations served in the officer's wardroom, where some of the finest sliders are conjured up for night-shift personnel.

"So you are — how shall I put this — the third-string Battle Watch?"

"Fourth. But at least I'm in the game. If anything big happens, I call the admiral on the batphone here." He pointed to a telephone without dials or numbers.

I looked at the large display screen. "Anything big happening now?"

He pointed to a contact in the upper-right corner of the screen. "See the merchant ship just south of Socotra? Charlie-foxtrot two-niner-niner?"

I nodded, picking out the vessel from a cluster of activity south of the Yemeni island.

"She's an arms merchant, illegal booty by international standards. We are tracking her for a possible takedown tomorrow. Or not. If the arms go to Iraq, we'll let her go. But if they steer toward Iran, something might happen. Right now, we just watch. That's my job, PB. Watch. And read." He sighed. "Read and watch. That's my sad, sorry life. Read and watch."

He picked up the red sheet-metal message board that held information culled from the cutters-and-pasters in the foyer. It was labeled TOP SECRET. "Here's what I wanted to show you." He handed me the board which was chock full of dot-matrixed naval messages. "Read the top two on the right side."

I read them and struggled to form an intelligent question. "If all the Soviet submarines are staying home, does that mean the Cold War is over?"

"I think it does," he replied. "But that doesn't mean peace on earth. More likely, it means hot wars and conflict in a whole lot of places that have unsettled issues. Iran and Iraq are already shooting at each other. India versus Pakistan is a powder keg ready to blow. And everybody over there always wants a piece of Israel."

"Should I change my orders to Pax? Extend my tour until the end of cruise?"

"Not necessary. Nothing is going to happen during this cruise. It's a good time to go learn some new stuff. Test pilot stuff, astronaut stuff. Hot wars will come later."

Those prophetic words had us both staring at the big screen for a long moment. Trash broke the silence. "I still smell it."

"Smell what?"

"The letter."

I pulled out Lori's letter and held it under his nose. He closed his eyes and sniffed. I took it away when he started moaning.

"Are you going to write back?" he asked. "You can beat the mail and call her from Diego Garcia. She's in Virginia, right? You can visit her before you start test pilot school."

"I'll write her back. I'm procrastinating right now, and I'm hungry. I might go to mid-rats and get a slider first."

Trash reached over to a shoebox next to the bat phone. "Skip mid-rats. Check these out." He opened the box to reveal individually wrapped white chocolate-chip macadamia cookies.

I stuffed one in my mouth and stashed two more in my flight suit for later. "I love Mrs. Trashman! She is such a cookie-meister."

"Mrs. Trashman," he sighed. "My wonderful Leslie. Oh, how I love her, too. She is the epitome of a domestic goddess." His eyes wandered but returned to the activity on the big screen. "Just imagine — she traded a career as an architect so I can do this."

That was my signal to leave, so I gave him a two-finger salute and departed. At the curtain, I heard a radio call from over the speakers and turned my attention back to his chair. The fourth-string battle watch officer picked up his handset and broadcast a message to all tactical assets deployed across the seas from the mightiest navy ship on the planet. "This is Alpha Bravo. Roger. Out." Trash looked back at me, and like Groucho Marx with a cookie instead of a cigar, bounced his eyebrows with a big, cheesy grin.

I went back to our stateroom.

> *Dear Lori,*
>
> *A wise and wonderful girl once told me that the secret to skating was to "never let go." That lesson extended far beyond the Woodland Hill Elementary School gym. My footing was uncertain then, and it wasn't just the skates. Today I am more confident in many of my abilities, but expressing love is not one of them. I will try my best.*
>
> *I just received orders to test pilot school. But that was the second-best thing I read today. Your letter was the tops. You were so honest with me, and you deserve honesty in return. I want to see you again, Lori. I want to see whether there is love in our future. We won't know for sure until we are together, and soon perhaps we will be. I will be leaving the ship in a day or two. Like you, I want to write down my feelings and emotions before my courage disappears.*
>
> *In previous letters, I may have projected that everything in my Navy life was perfect. If you are under the impression that everything comes easy for me, I assure you that it is not so. For example, I crashed on my first flight in the squadron. I suspect you already know about the incident from talking to my mom. It's not a story I like to retell, but I need to explain how important your advice was in my unfortunate adventure.*

After we hit the water, the aircraft turned toward my side of the cockpit leaving me strapped in my seat far from the surface and in almost complete darkness. As water gushed from above, panic surged from within. I released my harness. I floated out of my seat and floundered toward the back of the aircraft. I can't say for sure what I was thinking, but I know what I was doing. I was reaching, grasping for something to hold on to. And I found it. It was, of all things, a plastic tube that we pee into on long flights. It was still attached to a structural portion of the helicopter floor that was now the ceiling in an upside-down world. That piss-tube led me to an air pocket, and that air pocket gave me a second chance. I found a new grip on the sonarman's console, crawled hand-over-hand to the cabin door, and swam out of the sinking helicopter. Like you said, "Never let go." I didn't, and those words saved my life.

Lori, please listen to your own words. Do not let go. Do not let go of your brother, Michael. Do not let go of Patty, or your mom, or your dad, or the hope that your family will heal. If you need someone to remind you of these words, hold on to me. I can be that guy for you if you let me.

Maybe one day I will walk on the moon or fly a helicopter on Mars. But I would give all that up if I could bring Michael home to you. A helicopter is, above all else, a rescue vehicle. There is no higher honor than to be part of a crew that saves people. I want to be your rescue pilot, dear Lori. I want you in my helicopter.

I have some training to complete in Texas before I drive east to Pax River. After that, I want to meet you at Woodland Hill when the cicadas come back. I can't wait to see you.

Love, Peter

I breathed a deep sigh and opted not to re-read what I'd written. I found an envelope, addressed it to Lori in care of her sister, stamped it, and put it in the leg pocket of my flight suit.

4

1987
Woodland Hill, Virginia
Late May

By Memorial Day weekend, I had finished fixed-wing flight training in Corpus Christi, Texas, and was driving to southern Maryland to start test pilot school later in June. The timing to visit with Lori was perfect, at least for me. Most of my phone conversations regarding the visit were with Patty's message machine. Patty did return one call, explaining how busy Lori was with night school, an internship, and a part-time waitressing gig. I arranged the time and place for a rendezvous but dropped the ball on following up. My flight training in Texas was intense, and executing a move across the country distracted me from calling Lori directly. In hindsight, I should have asked Patty for more details about Lori's schedule.

Wanting to impress, I arrived early at Woodland Hill Elementary, wearing my flight suit. Did Lori remember our first kiss seventeen years before? Would the periodical cicadas trigger her memory? The fantastical insects from Brood X were omnipresent and loud, their emergence right on schedule.

Two people appeared outside of the school's rear fire exit. One was Patty for sure, but the other was not Lori. Patty embraced the other woman, said goodbye to her, and then walked my way. I waved and smiled, disguising my bemusement at Lori's absence.

"Peter!"

I gave Patty a hug. "It's good to see you."

"Look at you, so dashing in your uniform." She teared up. "You looked like Michael from a distance."

I had no good response, so I just shrugged.

"Lori's not coming," she blurted, her face flushed.

This whole matchmaking scheme was fraught with risk from the beginning, but I was still shocked.

"She wanted to be here," said Patty, "but she is flying out of the country. She was accepted into the Peace Corps and is on her way to her first assignment — an island called Vanuatu. Have you heard of it?"

"Near New Zealand," I said. "We sailed by it on my first cruise."

Patty must have read the gloom on my face. She motioned for both of us to sit in the grass. "I'm not a very good go-between for you two. You both are on the move all the time. If I had a telephone to take with me everywhere, I could have helped you two coordinate your schedules better."

"I owe you an apology, Patty. I asked you to set up our meeting because I was so busy in training. It was inconsiderate of me not to check in with Lori herself." I had never considered being stood up.

"Lori has been mapping a new career and sorting through some internal strife. The Peace Corps opportunity was a long time coming, but once she was accepted, things moved fast."

"I should have been there to support her."

"There are things you didn't know, Peter. Just between you

and me, Lori needed to go away." Patty sniffled and her face turned blotchy. "Last fall, we learned that our mom committed suicide. She had faded from our lives after the Vietnam War ended. Eventually, she shut us out."

I gasped. "Oh, God."

"Yeah, it was tough news to receive. Especially for Lori." Patty wiped her nose on her sleeve. "I can understand why she didn't tell you. Suicide is not something people like to talk about. Plus, Lori, more than anyone, tried hard to reach Mom, with the hope of at least maintaining contact. The news that she'd killed herself shattered Lori. Stacey and I are trying our best to put her back together." She pointed to the woman at the fire exit who was weeding the school's flower bed. "Stacey is the school counselor. She's my best friend." Her face wore a pained expression. "Check that, Peter," she said. "Stacey is my *girlfriend* and I should be proud to say it. She has been a great help to both Lori and me."

Patty took a deep, shaky breath. "Mom was a strong woman," she said. "Did you know she was a crane operator at the Norfolk Naval Shipyard during World War II?"

"I was a kid. I only knew her as your mom."

"She was a 'Rosie the Riveter' type. She 'manned' the cranes while Dad was in Europe. I went through her personal belongings and found their love letters that she had saved."

"Was that hard?"

"Hard, yes. But the letters were oh, so sweet. You remember Patch, right? Our one-eyed old codger of a father?"

"How could I forget Patch? I picked up Lori for a school dance once and asked him how he lost his eye in Korea. He told me he didn't lose it. He reached into his pocket and pulled out a marble and tossed it to me. I freaked out and almost threw up. I'd never seen Lori so mad at him."

Patty giggled. "Yup. That's my dad. He still carries that marble in his pocket. He pulled the same prank on Stacey."

"Go on," I said.

Patty nodded. "The Marine Corps assigned him to a base-security posting in England. He never ventured out of England and never experienced combat. On his return stateside, he proposed to my mom under the water tower over there." She pointed to the Woodland Hill landmark, and a cicada landed on her extended arm. She laughed. "These little guys were there when they had their first kiss. My dad referred to it in their letters.

"Once they were married, I think they both got restless here in town. My dad wanted to see combat, and my mom needed meaningful work. All the local jobs went back to the men returning home from the war. That was the beginning of Dad's Korean adventure and maybe the beginning of their troubles. They drove west to Camp Pendleton for combat training. Dad deployed with the 1st Marine Division to occupied China, while Mom found clerical work on the base. After Communist China sided with North Korea and invaded South Korea, the 1st Marines were sent in response. Daddy was a survivor of the battle for Chosin Reservoir."

"A brutal battle. Fought in subzero temperatures," I said.

"Yeah. He wanted to see combat. That he did. He was lucky that he only lost one eye." She paused for a breath. "They moved back here to convalesce and start a family. Pretend like the Korean War never happened."

"Well, it is referred to by some as 'The Forgotten War.'"

"But the fighting never stopped. The Koreans were still fighting when Michael was born. Thirty-five years ago today, May 25, 1952." She picked up a nearby cicada and watched as it crawled on her palm. "I was born one year later, May 31, 1953. Forever into eternity, Memorial Day will always fall either on one of our birthdays or between them."

I shook my head. "I didn't know your birthdays were so close."

"Yeah. It's painful to celebrate someone's birthday when you don't know if they're dead or alive. Oh, how I'd give anything to flip a hamburger for him at a Memorial Day barbecue. Or at least give me a cemetery plot to visit so I can plant a flower." She tossed the cicada in the air, and it flew off. "Amazing insects," she muttered.

"Noisy too," I said.

Patty smiled. "Cicadas always brought joy to Mom. She loved nature and things like that." She paused. "It makes no sense to me why she would give up and kill herself."

I put my hand on her shoulder. "Was it because of Michael?"

"You know, Stacey asked the same thing. She thinks Mom held herself responsible for Michael joining the Army. She loved the military life, even though she didn't serve herself. Dad, of course, was against him joining because of his Chosin experience. I remember the two of them fighting when Michael told them he was enlisting. The bickering continued well after he left for training."

"That must have been so hard on you and Lori."

"I'm telling you all this so that you know a little of what Lori is going through."

I leaned back in the grass and gestured for her to continue.

"Michael and I were a handful growing up, but because of us, Mom and Dad made the marriage work. Lori was born six years after me, causing Mom to switch gears from wanting to go back to work to childrearing again. It was divide-and-conquer parenting. Dad spent most of his time with Michael and me—that is, when he wasn't at the local veteran's lodge. Mom fawned over Lori, at least until the day the Army told us Michael was missing. The news changed all of us, but Lori and Mom's relationship was never the same. By March of 1973, Mom had had enough. The Vietnam POWs had just returned from Operation Homecoming and Michael was not aboard that last airplane. She left, and we rarely heard from her after that. Then we learned..." Patty let the sentence go unfinished as the cicadas screamed. She turned her attention to Stacey, who had just stood up from weeding the flower bed. Stacey waved. Patty smiled, then tugged at my flight suit. "I am cheering for you and Lori. I want you both to be happy, whether you are together or apart."

I picked up a cicada that had crawled onto my leg. "I was foolish to think that things between us could be like they were in our elementary school days."

"Not foolish!" Patty exclaimed, now in coaching mode. "We all have to deal with the circumstances we were born into. The good news is Lori is redefining herself. She is much more positive about the future, and I think you have a lot to do with it. Your letters picked her up when she was at her lowest. Now she has goals and a sense of purpose. Like you, she's embracing a career of service. She's going to teach people how to farm, read, start businesses. She'll have a job that demands hard work and hustle. She says that is the key to your success. I am proud of her for taking this opportunity."

"I think Michael would be proud, too."

"Now you're making *me* cry again," Patty said.

We basked in the cacophony of the cicadas, their calls to potential mates sounding louder and more desperate. Patty pulled a small note from her pocket. "Lori wanted me to give you this." She hugged me and then stood up. "I'll leave you alone to read it. You know where to find me. I'm not leaving Woodland Hill—this is where I belong. Please stay in touch, no matter what."

She jogged down the hill with a bunch of cicadas attached to the back of her pullover. Stacey greeted her with a bouquet from the flower bed. "Happy Birthday," I shouted. The two ladies waved back, blew kisses, and then disappeared into the school.

I opened the tightly packed triangle note from Lori.

> *Dear Peter,*
> *I love you.*
> *Lori*

Later that summer, I received a retention bonus from the Navy. They foolishly assumed money was necessary to keep me in service. I used the six thousand dollars to buy a Mac II personal computer—a gift to myself for test pilot school. One quiet evening, I resurrected my high school typing skills and set about digitizing the poems that I had written on deployment. In light of Lori's assignment to Vanuatu, the ending of one poem I had authored, titled "The Letter," felt a little too close to the mark.

The Letter

There is a Navy officer who is serving out at sea.
He flies a helicopter for the Indo-Pacific fleet.
Sometimes when he is feeling down or the pace is slow,
He wanders to the wardroom for a hot, brisk cup of joe.

There is a table in the wardroom where the pilot sits alone.
His friends are on duty, so his thoughts are all his own.
He leaves his coffee black, bringing the cup to his lip
while staring blankly at the wall of the haze-gray Navy ship.

There is a notepad in his pocket, a pen next to that.
He reaches for the pen and lays the notepad right out flat.
A glance at his watch face, he has some time to spare.
He sighs and takes one deep breath of cold and musty air.

There is a picture in his wallet of the girl that's on his mind.
He tries to write a letter, but the words are so hard to find.
He wants to tell her about his day and his job on that gray boat,
That portrays himself a hero who wishes not to gloat.

There is a pondering face: What word to conjure next?
How to mix emotion and inflection in the text?
Not wanting to be obvious, not wanting to be shy.
Not wanting to be truthful yet wanting not to lie.

There is coffee on the burner, he pours a second cup
And forces out one whole page, then lifts his head on up
to think about the nothings he has told this girl so far.
The time has come to make a move and catch a falling star.

There is a tension building as he poises with the pen.
Then the words all stumble out, beginning, middle, and end.
He writes to her the feelings that he harbors on this day
In just four simple, rhythmic lines. This is what they say:

Can you ever see the light shining through the storm?
    Can you ever feel the love behind a heart so torn?
    Can I ever lie with you and stay until the morn?
    Can I ever marry you and father your first born?

There is a call for the pilot, he is needed out on deck.
He reads once more the letter and says, "Oh, what the heck!"
He folds the letter gently and stashes it with his pen,
Thinking he will finish it when he gets a break again.

There is a certain irony when love seems so true,
yet separated but by miles, writing is all they do.
He wrote to her, "I love you." At least that's what he meant.
Why did he write such words in a letter never sent?

CYCLE THREE

Emergence

The mid-Atlantic Brood X cicadas from the genus *Magicicada septendecim* are 17-year periodicals that draw public attention for their springtime mass emergence in the adult stage of life. An individual cicada is a burrowed nymph for 95 percent of its existence, nourishing its growth from a tree's root. The cicada's adult stage is brief, with the sole purpose of mating. Scientists are divided over whether the prime-numbered-year periodical emergence is a byproduct of evolution or a clever strength-in-numbers survival tactic.

5

2004
The Pentagon, Arlington, Virginia
Saturday morning of Memorial Day Weekend

"Damn the inventor of the digital clock," I muttered as the dashboard flashed 9:11. White caps on the Potomac River appeared in my periphery.

I was driving north on the George Washington Memorial Parkway, having just left a heavenly embrace, and was now headed back to my routine hell. In past emotional breakdowns, I had felt no need to leave the car. Cry a few tears, wipe the sweat off, take a deep breath — it was procedure.

Not today. The river beckoned and I veered off to a parking lot along the Mount Vernon Trail. Called by the distant ocean downstream, I exited the car and strode toward the white foam. I stepped across a bike lane without looking or caring if a rider was coming at me. A dirt footpath took me to the river's edge. I remember the air being pungent from decayed fish littered below the tide line. Skyward, a murder of crows chased a hawk as he flailed in retreat.

At that moment, I considered a simple question: Why am I so sad?

The Potomac River's scum-topped surf offered no solace. I was in a far better place than the hawk and much better off than my Armed Forces colleagues stationed around the globe. I cried a few tears, took a deep breath, and leaned against a tree.

My sadness was interrupted when I spotted a familiar bug on the tree. The cicada—with its red eyes, large abdomen, and moist wings—had just emerged from a nymph shell. He was between stages, his newly metamorphized body free of its old carcass but not quite ready to fly in its new one.

I took the cicada as a sign to carry on. Whatever was eating me inside was gone. Returning to the car, I checked my face in the rear-view mirror and told myself, "You got this."

THE NAVY COMMAND CENTER ON the Pentagon's first floor had been rebuilt by the spring of 2004. My regular duties were in the D-wing on the fifth floor, where I served in a staff role for the Chief of Naval Operations in his Air Warfare Directorate. Monday through Friday, I fought a budget battle for the future of Navy helicopters. Every other weekend, I offered my services to an undermanned intelligence and operations watch overseeing Operation Iraqi Freedom, now in its second year. I volunteered to stand the watch as a tribute to the friends I lost on 9/11—and to fill a manpower gap. I had yet to un-volunteer.

The terrorist attack on the Pentagon was very personal. Not only was the attack on my place of work, but that day, 125 people died, including my best friend Mark, a.k.a. Trashman. Three years later, I had no way to honor his death other than offering to stand a few watches. Having finished the flying portion of my career at the turn of the millennium, I was now an office creature. "Read and watch" is how Trashman once described the monotony of intelligence, clearly downplaying his passion for the trade. He'd embraced the ever-increasing responsibility of spy craft throughout his career, just as I had done in aviation. When he left this earth, Trash was hardly the fourth-string intelligence officer he had jokingly referred to himself as on our first tour. His ghost, and those of his departed colleagues, haunted the new command center.

I was counting on his ghost to get me through another working weekend. At turnover, the off-going battle watch officer summed up the current operational picture for me.

"The cease fire in Najaf is not holding. There was a firefight in Kufa last night. Everything we do is, pardon my French, effed-up beyond all recognition. We're losing the war in Iraq. All naval units have been placed on high alert."

Just as baseball games are not won in the dugout, wars cannot be won from a headquarters in Washington, D.C. I was in the dugout for the war on terror. But the calculus changed when the petty officer of the watch informed me that Admiral Rasmussen had called earlier and wanted a callback. Razz, my former commanding officer, was now running a consulting firm in retirement. I found time about midway through my watch to return his call.

"PB, I have some gouge from the retired flag-officer network. You've been selected for a deep-draft command."

I was stunned. Not at being selected for command, but at being blindsided with a promotion announcement that I was not expecting until the next week. I was hardly prepared to respond, so I just said, "Thank you, sir. I'm honored."

Command-at-sea was the next rung on a career ladder I continued to climb. It meant I would be assigned as an executive officer and then commanding officer of a helicopter-carrying amphibious assault ship. The ship and crew belonged to the Navy. The helicopters and flight crew were the property of the Marine Corps.

Razz cut through my BS. "Don't sound so thrilled."

"I'm sorry, sir. I *am* honored. It's just that I wasn't expecting to hear the news until next week. And I'm on duty. The war is not going so great."

He sighed. "Yes, I know." I assumed he was up to speed on the current situation in Iraq. "I'm sorry if the timing is off. But you should know what to expect from the Navy bureaucracy next week. A high-ranking puke from the personnel bureau is going to call you and lay on a whole lot of patriotic crap. Of course, they want you to drive their ship. You are the best of the best in naval aviation. But senior service has a cost. It's three years of sea duty max. And the Marines are fighting wars again, so you'll be in the thick of it. Deep-draft command is a guaranteed path to admiral if you don't screw up. Your personal life will take a big hit though. I want you to be prepared for that."

"Therein lies my problem, Razz."

"What's that, son?"

"My personal life is all messed up." I rubbed the bridge of my nose and looked around to see if any of the watchstanders were in hearing range.

Razz gave me a moment to recover and continued the conversation. "Then I'm glad I called. Now you have forty-eight hours or so to take personal inventory. It's time I didn't have when I accepted orders for deep draft. I don't regret serving the amphibious Navy. In fact, I'm proud to be a 'frog' as they say. But being a frog will only get you so far in the promotion game. And the cost to your quality of life is substantial. Times haven't changed, PB."

"Thanks for the career advice, Admiral."

"The advice is cheap. What I really care about is you. I'll let you go back to watch and take care of business. Promise me you'll call if you need to talk things out. I've been in your shoes, son. But they fit you better."

"Thanks, Razz." I hung up the phone and returned to monitoring the war. I muddled through the next hour or so, listening in on planning briefs that were six time zones away. I updated the color-coded assessment charts on the secret computer share-drive. All indicators of the war's success were sliding backward from warning yellow to code red. "Life sucks," I mumbled, then set out for a head call and a coffee break.

At the coffee mess, I reached for powdered cream but paused as my hand brushed a plastic spice shaker of cinnamon. My mind jumped to Lori. Would talking to her make me feel better? I knew from our yearly Christmas card exchange that she was trotting the globe on behalf of the US Agency for International Development. The Pentagon had a new email system with a global directory that included all federal agencies. I found her contact information and composed a simple inquiry.

P: Hi Lori. It's Peter. Is this a good email address? No business. Just want to catch up. I hope all is well.

I stepped away from the keyboard for a moment to ponder what I had just written. "Oh hell," I said under my breath as I clicked the SEND button. Minutes later, I received a reply.

> L: OMG, Peter! Where in cyberspace have you been? Yes, this is a good email. The Earthlink address in the copy line is even better. But better yet is my phone number! Even more better is an in-person visit!! You are a man of so few words. Where are you? When can we talk? I'll stop now. You have so made my day. Call me! XOXOXO, Lori
>
> P: Can't call right now. On duty at the Pentagon. Tonight?
>
> L: Pentagon! Holy crap, you scoundrel!! I'm across the river at Foggy Bottom, training for my next assignment. I'm staying with Patty while I'm back in town. Here for a week more and then off to Sri Lanka. So much to tell you. Let's ditch the phone call. How about a face to face? ;-) Does tomorrow morning sound good? I also have Monday off. I can drive your way to Arlington.
>
> P: I need to get out of town. Can we meet at Woodland Hill?
>
> L: Yes, I love it! Our spot?

I smiled, then typed.

> P: Perfect...like you.
>
> L: :-)

"Captain?" The petty officer of the watch poked his head into my cubicle. "The Fifth Fleet operational update brief starts in five minutes."

"Copy that," I replied. I typed my last email to Lori for the day.

> **P: Got some duty-scheduling issues on my end. Is Monday morning okay?**
>
> **L: Anytime is good. Just let me know. You made my day!**

I sighed and refocused on the Fifth Fleet operational update.

WAKING UP EARLY WAS NOT a problem, even after Sunday night's watch. In command, I had learned to structure a demanding day around chaos and near persistent interruption. Erratic sleep was the norm. On that tour, I immersed myself in the lives of my sailors, especially during flight operations. My senior enlisted command chief worried that I didn't trust my troops, and my executive officer was concerned about his own career. What some would call micro-management, I called leadership. I watched over my sailors as Razz had watched over me. I cared for them as individuals — not as the ranks on their sleeves. Nobody crashed on my watch, not in helicopters or in off-duty traffic accidents. Like the catcher I was, I trained them to master their fields of responsibility. I told them, "Don't let the ball get by you." None of them did.

My helicopter squadron was thrust into the role of the aircraft carrier's primary defensive weapon when, in the year 2000, a bomb-carrying terrorist boat rammed the USS Cole during a refueling stop in Yemen at Aden Harbor. We anticipated similar small-boat attacks as our battle group patrolled the troubled waters of the Arabian/ Persian Gulf. I made sure our squadron was ready for any challenge and led them to the pinnacle of operational readiness. We flew our asses off on that cruise, and I learned how to live in a world where sleep was a luxury.

6

2004
Woodland Hill, Virginia
Memorial Day

As I drove into the Woodland Hill Elementary School drop-off circle, I passed by signage that identified Michelle Myers as the principal. "Wow,'" I said out loud, trying to do the math in my head for the number of years it had been since I had read or heard that name. The signage triggered a memory of our sixth-grade skating party. The same trepidation and nerves I'd had that night accompanied me in the car today.

I hadn't seen Lori in eight years. We had crossed paths in Monterey, California, when I attended an aviation safety course on the Naval Postgraduate School campus. She was posted to the Defense Language Institute at the Presidio, gaining proficiency in what I remember was her third non-native language. We only had a few days of reacquaintance before she'd embarked on her first Foreign Service Officer assignment with the Department of State. I remember talking about our mutual wish-list for matrimony, though it was more like playful banter about what characteristics we desired in a potential mate.

The lure of the baseball diamond got me out of the car. I walked to the backstop, which, like me, was in desperate need of repair. Yellow caution tape was haphazardly tied to the sharp edges of the chain link that had dislodged from its support poles.

Lori appeared from the wooded path that led to her old neighborhood—where Patty now lived. As we embraced, I felt eleven years old again. We held hands and walked through a pockmarked, anthill-infested left field toward the tree-lined school boundary. No words. Just smiles as we sauntered to our familiar spot on the ridge next to the trees. We sat in the untamed grass.

She spoke first. "I'm so glad you found me. You look good."

"And you look perfect."

"Why, thank you." She blushed. "I just might add you to my list of suitors. Please do go on."

"Sri Lanka sounds exciting. I did a port call in the capital city, Colombo, on my third cruise."

"What can I say? I'm a career girl. I'll be the agency's rep on the embassy team. It's the next rung on the ladder for me. You?"

"More sea time is coming my way. I was promoted and will be offered command of a helicopter transport ship. I'm not sure I want it."

"Sounds like a big deal. What's stopping you?"

I listened to the chorus of cicadas hollering from the trees and waved my arm around, ending with it pointed at the Woodland Hill playground. "This. A normal life. A wife. A boring job. A hobby. Kids."

"Sounds like a shopping list."

"I'm forty-five years old. I'm in a bit of a mid-life crisis."

"So, shopping for a wife solves the problem?"

"Maybe."

"Am *I* on your list?"

"You've always been at the top."

"Aha! You finally admit that you have a list!"

I could only smile.

Lori brushed back her hair and looked away. "Well, if I'm on the top of that list, you better renew your passport, pal. Nothing is going to be normal with me."

"Miss Myers said as much in sixth grade," I retorted with a laugh. "Did you see that she's the principal?"

"Yes. Patty is a classroom teacher at the school now. Her partner, Stacey, is the school district's counselor. They want to get married but same-sex marriage is still illegal in Virginia." She paused. "Stupid policy. Patty is quite the activist, though. She's teaching me how to be a muckraker and affect change without excess expenditure of emotion. It's a skill I'll need to master in the diplomatic corps."

"I wish we had the same-sex thing figured out in the Navy," I replied. "I've lost too many good sailors to administrative processes. Important social issues like marriage rights, civil rights, even the environment tend to go by the wayside in a war."

She smiled pensively. "There's always going to be a war, Peter. Normal life only exists on TV. You won't find it because it is not real." Her words reminded me that I was talking to a Gold Star family member, the sister of a soldier still MIA.

The cicadas were flying now, which made me think of our first kiss back in 1970. It was enough to put me in a mood of openness and vulnerability. "I lost my best friend on September 11. I'm not over it, and I don't know what to do."

She reached for my hand. "You'll never get over it, Peter. You will carry the loss with you forever. But over time, it won't be so heavy, especially if you let a friend help you carry the burden." That had not been the response I was expecting. She squeezed my hand as my tear ducts opened.

"Tell me about that day, Peter. Tell me everything."

I shook my head. "Where do I start? I was looking forward to a traditional cup of coffee with Trashman. You remember my roommate from my first tour?"

"Trashman? Of course." She smiled. "You Navy guys and your call signs. In all your letters and in what you told me about Mark, I know he kept you safe and sane on deployment. I love Trashman." She referred to him in present tense, just like when she talked about Michael.

"Well, that day he was in the Navy Command Center on the first floor of the Pentagon. My office was—and still is—on the fifth floor. Trash was the command center section head, the senior intelligence officer. Because everybody worked for him, he could step out for meetings or coffee anytime. On a normal day, he would ring me up around 7:30. If I was free, we'd meet on the third floor in the stairwell and walk to the Starbucks kiosk. I say, 'normal day,' but there is hardly ever a normal day in the Pentagon."

"Or in Washington, D.C., for that matter," Lori said.

I stepped through the timeline of my trauma to describe what happened. "Trash called me at 7:30 to ask for a push until 8:30. Something was going on in the background, but he gave no clue what it was. That was fine by me because K-dog, my old executive officer, was coming by for a meeting.

"K-dog worked for the prime manufacturer of our fleet helicopters. I remember how thrilled I was that the three of us were going to swap sea stories from the old days. Trashman and I knew each other's stories all too well. Our routine was starting to get monotonous. A visit from K-dog was a welcome change." A tear rolled down my cheek as I spoke. "Now I wish to holy hell that boredom would rise up and return to my life."

Lori leaned against me. "Keep going. Tell me more."

"K-dog was prompt. At 8:30, we were at my desk in the center of the cubicle farm in the D-wing, fourth corridor, very near the windows that looked out at the outermost E-ring. Sometime close to the top of the hour, we heard a commotion from the jet jocks. They were watching TV, and the first plane had hit the north World Trade Center tower. K-dog and I joined the folks around the TV as the second plane hit the south tower. No one talked. We were all senior officers. Many of us had just returned from sea duty and knew who Al Qaeda was." I paused to take a breath, remembering.

"Mind you, my job in the office was to plan future helicopter budgets for the Chief of Naval Operations. We were trying to defend money for programs that wouldn't be implemented for five or six years. Nothing we did in that office would help the current fleet fight any enemy attack. We fought for the future.

"But that morning, we were punched in the present, and we had no way to respond. Everyone around the TV understood who did it and what type of military response would be required. No one said a word until our always smiling Chief of Staff came in stone-faced and said he was headed to the Navy Command Center to find out what was going on.

"I looked at K-dog and said, 'Let's call Trashman.' We walked back to my cubicle. By now, it was close to 9:30. K-dog suggested Mark might be too busy to answer, so I asked him to pardon me while I called my parents. He went back toward the jet jocks. By instinct, I dialed my brother's number, knowing that I only had time for one phone call. This was not news my parents could handle without Jason's help. Unfortunately, I got his answering machine. I remember saying, 'Jason, turn on the TV and give me a call.'"

Lori pulled a thermos from her handbag. Not saying a word, she poured me a cup of lukewarm coffee. My hand shaking, I took a sip, put the cup aside, and took some deep breaths, a calming technique that worked for me in flight school. More cicadas were flying around. Their emergence from the trees, their shouts for mates, and their chaotic flight soothed me. I laid back in the grass and closed my eyes.

"I had been in an earthquake before. I felt tremors a few times in San Diego. Seattle, too. When the floor in my office shifted below my feet, that's what I thought it was.

"The first thing I did was stand. I checked my footing and looked around. Our directorate was in a newly renovated portion of the Pentagon. My view from the west-facing windows was the outer E-ring of the Pentagon. The windows were designed to withstand a truck bomb blast, a lesson learned from the attack at the Khobar Towers Air Force dorm complex in Saudi Arabia—and they did their job that morning. What I saw was yellow—a complete fireball. But for some reason, even though planes hit the towers in New York, I assumed a truck bomb had hit us.

"Once the fireball passed, the office lights went dark. I remember touching myself, patting my chest as if I had to reassure myself that

I was not hit. I remember thinking, 'I am still alive. I am well. I can help.'"

Lori placed her hand on my chest and scooted closer to me. I kept my eyes closed.

"The darkest part of the office was farthest from the door. Navy training kicked in, and I started a search for anyone who needed help. Funny though, the entire office was filled with trained officers. Everyone was doing the same thing. Some of the cubicle walls had toppled, so I checked under a few for anybody that might be pinned or hurt. Smoke was accumulating below the ceiling tiles. I wasn't analyzing anything at this point. I was extremely calm. I suppose it was adrenaline. You know, fight or flight." I opened my eyes to see hers locked on mine.

She whispered. "Keep going."

"It was a Marine Corps officer—one of the colonels from the Corps' aviation branch. He yelled, 'We got everybody. Get the fuck outta here!' I followed his orders and joined the flow of people lining up to get out the door and leave the building. No one was running. We were like well-behaved school kids practicing a fire drill.

"I remember exiting the office and thinking about where to go. The group was turning left and heading toward the lights that illuminated the center ring where the escalators were. 'Head toward the light.' That's what we were taught. That's how you get out of a sinking helicopter. It works for burning buildings too." I chuckled at my morbid attempt at humor.

"I love that Marine," she said.

"Me, too. I mean those guys are the best in crises." I rolled over on my stomach, watching a cicada on its back, wiggling its legs, struggling to right itself. I flipped him over and watched as he marched away.

"What happened next?" said Lori. "Obviously, you got out."

"I guess this is where I have trouble. My mind keeps flashing to the stairwell outside my office that goes down to the command center—where Trashman and I would meet on the third floor. I remember thinking, 'I should go down that stairwell. Somebody there needs my help.'

"In retrospect, the stairwell might have already been destroyed. The airplane had plowed through the outer E-ring and torn through the D-ring below us. The first and second floors were consumed, the third heavily damaged. The fourth floor and *my* floor, the fifth, were somehow still stable. We were in the best shape to help anybody who needed it. Maybe there was someone in the stairwell. Maybe our chief of staff, maybe Trashman."

Lori let me feel sorry for myself only briefly. She looked down and shook her head. "Trashman wasn't in that stairwell. He's like you. He was probably trying to help the people around him—his sailors, his fellow officers, his civilian staff. The janitor, for goodness sake. I know from your letters that Mark was that kind of guy. He'd have given his life for the fellow next to him. He's like you, Peter."

"You're right, of course," I said. "And, in the moment I was contemplating the stairwell, a woman screamed. There was blood on the face of a coworker next to me. I pulled a handkerchief from my back pocket and told him, 'Bobby, you're bleeding. Let me put this on your head.' Bobby looked dazed as we moved like cattle toward the escalators. I grabbed his arm and told him, 'I'm your buddy today, Bobby. Walk with me. I'll get you to medical. I'm not leaving you.' And I didn't. I walked with Bobby on my arm to the escalator. We walked down to the first floor and exited outside to the center courtyard. Bobby held the hanky on his gash, and I led him to where we could sit him down and call for medical help."

"Typical you," she said. "You do all this stuff to help people and then you bury it. Did you ever tell your mom this story?"

"I told my dad before he died last year. I try not to burden Mom with my problems."

"She's stronger than you give her credit for. I call her every now and then to check up on you. But keep talking. Tell me what happened next."

"We got lost. We were in the center courtyard, thinking we were safe, but folks were screaming for us to keep moving toward the ninth corridor—toward the east exit and the north parking lot. We joined another pack of people and headed in that direction. I was the de facto leader of this small group, but somehow, I led them into a dead end. We ended up in a maintenance corridor and had to go back to the courtyard. I guess in the confusion somebody figured out where we were and led us the right way. Bobby was holding up well and I was focused on finding him a medical technician.

"Once in the ninth corridor, we met uniformed personnel who told us to keep going. They were the Defense Protective Service, DPS. The Pentagon's dedicated police force. Good guys. Thoroughly in control. We shuffled with the crowd out the E-ring exit and there I recognized a few of Bobby's colleagues from our office: Jimmy and Owen. 'Over here, PB,' they yelled. They took Bobby from me and led him toward the highway, where a good Samaritan drove him to a hospital."

"How was he after it was all over?"

"Bobby took a brick to his head during the blast. The gash needed a few stitches. He was awarded a Purple Heart after the president declared September 11 the first day of the War on Terror." I chuckled. "I think what Bobby appreciated more was the autographed construction helmet Jimmy and Owen gave him at his retirement ceremony last month."

"You work with some great people."

"Yes, I do. Speaking of great people, K-dog and I met after I handed Bobby off. He was in the same crowd that came out on the north side of the building. We looked at each other and said, 'We've got to go back inside.' We ran toward the entrance that we had just come out of, but DPS blocked us from going back into the building. 'Get out.' they yelled. 'Get everyone out of here! There's another one coming.' I think that's the first time I realized that the Pentagon had been hit by an airplane. And that there might be more airplanes crashing. Like in Shanksville, Pennsylvania."

I was shaking, and Lori cuddled me. "They were heroes. Flight 93, the crew, the passengers. All heroes like you."

I shook my head. "I'm not a hero, Lori. Just a catcher trying not to let the ball get by."

"Let's drink more coffee. Let's watch the bugs. Let's take a break from that day," she said, offering me an out. But I needed to tell her more, and she knew I needed to talk.

"We had quite the journey getting home. After running stretchers and shuffling medical supplies from one side of the Pentagon to the other, K-dog and I hit the road and walked north toward Rosslyn. We had to walk. DPS locked down the parking lot so we couldn't get to our cars. The Army base at Fort Meyer and Arlington National Cemetery were locked down, too. We walked the vacant highways like war refugees. We talked and processed what had just happened. Two other officers joined us. None of our cellphones worked that day—the network was jammed from overuse. I don't know how long it took, but I remember emerging from the highway at the Marine Corps Memorial. The Iwo Jima statue. God, what a surreal experience."

"As I said, I love Marines," said Lori. "They led you out of the darkness and into the light."

"And to an apartment complex, where some very nice people took us in, gave us water, and let us use their landline telephones. I still had Bobby's blood on my khaki uniform. A nice lady offered me her boyfriend's sweatshirt, but I wouldn't take it. I wanted to stay in uniform."

"Who did you call?"

"Jason, of course. He would let Mom and Dad know I was okay. After that, I called Mark's wife, Leslie. Up to that point, I had been avoiding thinking about Trashman. Eventually, it sank in. Leslie said he hadn't called home. I told her about the cellphone jams, the traffic snarls, and the general chaos of the mass evacuation. I was hoping a hospital would call her soon to say her husband was a patient. But the image of the stairwell door flashed into my head—the darkness. Somehow, I knew then that my best friend was one of the many who would be on the casualty list."

I stood up to stretch my legs. "Is this too much, Lori? I haven't seen you in such a long time, and here I am, pouring out nothing but hurt, pain, and agony."

"We were all there, Peter. Yes, you were in the middle of the blast and have a unique story. But we were all there. And I want you to tell me everything. I leaned on you when I was having my doubts about, well, let's just say life itself. Lean on me, Peter."

I wandered over toward the tree line and flicked the empty shell of a cicada from a tall white oak. "This is a very calming place," I said. "I liked living here." I turned and scanned the landscape down the hill and toward the horizon, taking in the dilapidated ball field, the pittance of a playground, the school, the water tower. "I like coming here. I feel much better now."

"But you can't stay, Peter. You can stop by on occasion. Patty and her partner, Stacey, will always be here. They will always welcome you. But you have places you need to be."

"I have something else I want to tell you," I said. "I mean about that day."

"And I have something to tell you. Completely different topic. You go first."

"Okay, I'll go first. That day of the attack, when I patted my chest after the fireball, I was also checking for this." I reached into my jeans pocket, pulled out the POW/MIA bracelet, and handed it to her.

Lori gasped. She clutched the bracelet, curling into a ball as tears flowed down her cheeks. I helped her up off the ground and held her in my arms. It took more than a moment for words to return. I gave her my handkerchief.

"There's more to this story, Lori."

"Tell me."

"I've had this bracelet since seventh grade. My mom gave it to me. She said I should never forget our soldiers and the sacrifice they were making for our country. I think I was too young to understand. I kept it because it was yet another reminder of you."

"I love you, Peter." She squeezed me harder.

"I have to admit, Lori, that over time, the bracelet became my lucky charm. It was something I had to have with me or near me all the time. But the bracelet is a poor substitute for the real thing."

"What do you mean?"

"Through my work in the Pentagon, I learned about a defense agency that deals with personnel recovery. That's what we call search and rescue these days. There's an office in Crystal City that handles prisoner of war and missing personnel issues. I met with their folks, and I think you or Patty should call them. They are sending teams to Vietnam. I'm sure they have a file on Michael, but access is only granted to direct family members. These are the guys that can help us find your brother."

A tear rolled down her cheek. "I don't know what to say." She paused. "You've given me renewed hope, Peter. I want him back. I want Michael back."

I released her from our embrace. "Hang tight. I'll be right back." I sprinted down the ridge to the backstop of the baseball field. I tore a long strip of yellow caution tape from the mangled metal and raced back to Lori. "Come with me."

She took my hand, and I led her to the tree line at the top of the ridge. A few yards in, I found a juvenile eastern black oak. "Help me tie this," I said.

We wrapped the tape twice around the trunk chest high. I tied the ends with a bow, and we stepped back onto the grass. "That's for Michael...until he comes home."

She leaned against me heavily as we stared into the wood. Then she sighed. "I am running out of tears."

"That's good," I said. "It's time to stop crying. For Trashman. For Michael. We should remember them, but the crying should stop." I put my arm around her. "Now tell me what *your* news is."

She straightened up, threw her hair back, and looked me square in the eye. "I am having a baby."

"You're pregnant?"

"No. No," she said, giggling. "I am adopting a baby boy. I am going to raise him myself."

"A boy?"

"A boy. He's from Korea. I'm working with an overseas adoption agency to get through some legal entanglements, but I received news Friday that I have been approved. I'm going to be a mom."

I smiled. "You are going to be a great mother. That is such wonderful news! I am so happy for you."

"There is more."

"Bring it on."

"I know my son will need a male role model as he grows up. Peter, I want you to be that man. What I'm asking is, will you play a major role in my son's life?"

Beaming, I threw my arms around her and said without hesitation, "Count on it!"

As I drove the George Washington Parkway toward the Pentagon for duty late that Memorial Day afternoon, I blared a CD through the car speakers and sang along with Bruce Springsteen at the top of my lungs. For the first time in a long time, I felt good about who I was and where I was going. And that was deep-draft command-at-sea. Before making the phone call to accept the orders, I dusted off a poem that helped me make sense of my station in life.

Kudos for the Sailor

Where there is tragedy, there is triumph;
the two seem to always coexist.
Nowhere is this more evident
than on a mighty Navy ship.

When seconds count on the flight deck
or in a main-space fire below,
professionals meet the challenge
routinely—without flash or show.

The standard is set every day;
training is a sailor's guide.
When pay is often not enough,
the sailor runs on pride.

Let fear stay with the homestead,
for no sailor fears the sea,
no pilot fears the atmosphere,
no submariner fears the deep.

Triumph over tragedy.
Professional, not possessed.
Patriotic, not fanatic.
Shipmates above all else.

7

2012
The Pentagon, Arlington, Virginia
Autumn

I was early for my performance evaluation with the Vice Chief of Naval Operations, so I stopped by the rebuilt fourth-corridor, third-floor coffee shop where Trashman and I had routinely met more than a decade ago. A double-shot espresso got my juices going. My mind strayed to the myriad of professional opportunities that lay ahead of my expected second-star promotion and the personal sacrifices I might have to confront.

In 2009, Lori and her six-year-old son Charlie had been pierside to greet me as I walked down the gangplank of my amphibious assault ship for the last time as commanding officer. My crew had just returned from the Persian-Arabian Gulf, where we supported elements of the 1st Marine Division and coalition special forces in Afghanistan. At dinner, I relayed to her many of my personal observations about Operation Enduring Freedom.

Then she hit me with the news that she had volunteered to join the US embassy team in Kabul, Afghanistan. Hardship tours, she rationalized, would compensate for her late-career start in the

Foreign Service. In that moment, I discarded the romantic fantasies I had harbored while deployed. It was clear to me that we were both uncompromising careerists who shared the burden of war. We served the national security enterprise and were concurrently prisoners of its trauma. Missions requiring our skills and experience would send us to far regions of the globe—and we would never be in the same place at the same time.

She would go on to serve on the Female Engagement Team in the Farah Province throughout 2010. Never a hangar queen, she disdained the comfort and safety of the embassy compound and quickly became the Farah leader. I started 2010 by pinning on a star to become a Rear Admiral and assumed a leadership billet at the Naval Research Laboratory in Anacostia under the Office of Naval Research (ONR). I also signed papers *in loco parentis* as Charlie's legal guardian while Lori was deployed.

I loved my tour as a research boss. My test pilot credentials and my technology-savvy brother made me a good fit for the billet. Jason, at the time, was a rising entrepreneur in Silicon Valley with a substantial bandwidth for innovation. My focus at the lab was on shiny objects—commercial sensor hardware with military applications. I needed Jason's perspective to balance sales pitches from persistent congressional lobbyists and the Beltway Bandits, the name given to the plethora of military-industrial contractors around D.C.

Though I was on shore duty, work-related travel was unavoidable. But most of the trips were short and domestic, which allowed me to play the substantial role in Charlie's life that Lori had asked of me. Though not a parent myself, I empathized with the struggles of deployed families. I did the best I could for Charlie, who lived with me and stayed with his aunts, Patty and Stacey, when I traveled.

Lori and I had a shared sense of duty to save the world, but neither of us had a clue to what that meant and even less of an idea about what our relationship was or should be. But we had Charlie — and Lori and I were dedicated to raising this beautiful son of Korea. My most important job in 2010 was making sure Charlie knew he was loved by his deployed mother. My second most important job was making sure Charlie made it to baseball practice on time.

Though I wore the rank of admiral, I was just another single-working parent in the suburbs of northern Virginia. Needing help with simple things like transportation, I overcame my past awkwardness and called Leslie, Trashman's widow. Despite her own parenting burdens, she was more than happy to help with Charlie's baseball practice drop-offs and snack schedule obligations.

We developed a routine around weekend youth events, chores, and shopping. Our time spent together helped me to appreciate the soul of this woman Trashman had called a "domestic goddess." Leslie was the architect of young people's lives. She was the master designer of the moral compass her girls navigated by. She was a leader by example — president of the Parent Teacher Association, treasurer for the neighborhood swimming team, and a key online organizer for the region's network of military spouses. In short, she was the commanding officer of the home front. As awesome as the view is from those heights, it can also be lonely at times.

In 2011, Lori returned from her one-year tour in Afghanistan and immediately accepted a posting with the State Department in Seoul, South Korea. Naturally, this time, she took Charlie with her.

Without Charlie to look after, I immersed myself in Leslie's world.

I helped her daughters financially and provided a lot of coaching, mentorship, and fatherly advice I had no qualifications to give.

Then one night, I accepted a dinner invitation from Leslie. Her girls were away at school. I drove straight to her house from work and stayed much longer than I expected. After the dishes were cleaned, we watched a romantic comedy while nestled on the couch. I felt welcome, safe, and at home.

Eight years before, Leslie's "heavenly embrace" had tugged on a thread of my moral fabric. Whether it was or wasn't, sleeping with my best friend's widow had felt like adultery. We had been two mature adults, consenting — and confused. That was no longer true.

Lori gave me her blessing when we talked by phone a few nights later. "You always wanted a normal life," she reminded me, and then paused. "But I sense there's more you're not saying about Leslie."

"We are close. And getting closer."

"Does that frighten you?"

"No. But it still seems wrong somehow."

"It seems very right to me."

"Do you approve?"

"You don't need my approval." She paused. "Do you love her?"

"I *do* love her."

"I bet she loves you."

"It's complicated."

And it was. But in the winter of 2011, I found the nerve to ask Leslie for her hand and became a husband. We married quietly in the spring of 2012 and adopted Katya — a conflict orphan from Ukraine who would fill a void, keeping us both from becoming empty nesters when Charlie left and Mark's daughters were no longer in the house. By fall of that year, my personal life and career were going great.

But Razz, my old skipper and mentor, had been right when he told me that flag officer promotions were political. Doing a good job matters less than being in the right place, next to the right person, at the right time. Pedigree also matters. Navy helicopter pilots rarely get a second star.

The Navy values its ships, submarines, and aircraft, but among the latter, jets rule, and jet pilots always migrate to the top ranks. The vice chief — a jet pilot himself — was respectful and polite as I entered his E-ring Pentagon office. He first congratulated me on Katya's adoption and then told me not to expect a promotion.

Although no civilian would pity a passed-over admiral, I was shocked. The blow to my ego was real and painful. At the time and across the fleet, over sixty of my peers were under investigation or were being indicted for scandals ranging from adultery to bribery and corruption. How could they not promote me? I had played the game fair my whole Navy career. This was not an outcome I had planned on.

Polishing the turd he had just handed me, the vice asked, "Where would you like to end your career, PB?" Although disappointed, I instantly knew the answer. While at Navy Research, I had occasionally accompanied Patty on visits to the offices of the Defense POW/MIA Accounting Agency (DPAA) in Arlington. She not only represented her family but also became an internet ambassador for several other families. Those visits helped me establish a friendship with the agency deputy — also a passed-over one-star admiral — who managed the portfolio of soldiers who were missing in action. He had asked for my advice on how technology could aid his search for missing persons from World War II—his highest priority. He also shared his intent to retire soon and asked for my brother's contact information.

He knew more than I did about Jason's work with artificial intelligence. As an exploitable maritime capability, Jason's technology was interesting, but I shied away from any direct outreach to avoid nepotistic misperceptions, conflicts of interest, or violations of acquisition law. I maintained a focus on hardware—an exciting portfolio of advanced sensors that penetrated walls, tree canopies, and ocean surf. But did I play the game too safe? In the plush E-ring office opposite the second-most senior officer in the Navy, I squirmed in my chair.

The vice's executive assistant entered the office, diverting his short attention span toward three red-hot pieces of paper that required his signature. While the two conferred, I stole a glance out the west-facing window toward Arlington National Cemetery. My bitterness waned when I eyed the autumn trees in the distance. A sprinkling of white headstones shone through the half-filled red oaks and orange maples. The headstones were aligned but for one bare spot in an otherwise flawless formation. I imagined myself standing over this bare spot, staring at a freshly installed headstone—that of Michael's. For the first time in my career, I got to choose my next job. I was a catcher again, calling the next pitch.

As the executive assistant left the room, I gave my answer to the vice chief. "I hear the one-star missing-persons billet at DPAA is coming available. With your concurrence, I would like to take that billet. I'll serve to high-year tenure in 2015. I have some ideas and programs I'd like to try."

"That works for me, PB. I'll make it happen." He shook my hand to conclude the meeting. "Who knows? I could be your boss if my assignment to the Joint Staff is approved." He grinned at me. "I would like that."

Before I left the Pentagon, I returned to the third-floor coffee shop. A caramel macchiato did little to calm my nerves as I thought of Leslie, Katya, Lori, and Charlie. What had I just signed up for?

8

2015
Mission Michael

Much to Leslie's dismay, I traveled more as a deputy at DPAA than as a boss at ONR. I went overseas to the places where soldiers last fought and were never seen again. I visited my agency counterparts in Russia, Iraq, Korea, and Southeast Asia, laying the groundwork for future repatriation efforts, codifying intelligence-sharing and mission-reconstruction agreements.

I also traveled to a few of the soldiers' hometowns to meet with their grieving families. I immersed myself in their stories and directed my staff to do the same. Since 1941, over 81,000 service members that had been engaged in armed conflicts were still missing or otherwise unaccounted for. Michael was one such soldier. I used my connection with his family to motivate me and my guidance to staff, though I tried not to make him my singular focus. That would be unethical at best, abuse of authority at worst. Despite these concerns, I labeled the project folder on my computer "Mission Michael."

The numbers themselves demanded a better system to find clues as to a service member's location. I used every tool I had at my disposal for this quest. The Navy had finally opened a portfolio on computer machine learning, a research program I had encouraged but could not fund. The Defense Department was still struggling to convince high-tech companies to embrace the military as a partner. My job required that I build a bridge between those two empires.

Taking a break from work one weekend, Leslie and I visited Patty. Over dinner, Stacey's dissertation came up. "Give us the thirty-second synopsis of what you've learned, Stacey," Leslie said.

Stacey laughed. "You want me to boil down five years of my life into thirty seconds?" We all smiled and she finally conceded.

"Okay, here it goes. Narrative helps us understand human behavior. Put in layman's terms, storytelling can reveal clues to a person's intrinsic motivation."

"So you are saying that reconstructed narrative can reveal a past behavior?" I asked.

"It all depends on what you *mean* by behavior."

In a lively debate over dessert, we agreed to define behavior as the result of a person's decisions, based on limited choices and influenced by external circumstances.

As we drove home, I asked Leslie what she thought about Stacey's research. Could a soldier's choices be mapped by their previous experiences? She agreed that she thought it was possible.

At work on Monday, I contracted a study that confirmed the hypothesis: clues to an individual's future behavior exist in stories about their pasts. Context—time, place, mood, etc.—can predict a future decision or the probability of arrival at some esoteric location—even a physical location, if provided enough cogent details. And those details come from people who know them best.

Mission Michael became an effort to mine historical narratives from veterans of a particular conflict. We projected the data quantity would be enormous and the computer bill for data processing to be expensive. A small-scale feasibility study was needed to sharpen the technical tools and to capture the realistic costs. I contracted another study focusing just on World War II. Starting with a group of veterans from the European theater, the study team captured data from the memories of aging heroes. They applied data analytics to narrow the range of probabilities of where soldiers' remains might be on a terrain map.

The World War II results were promising but lacked a grounding in brain science. I shared our progress with Stacey, who suggested I contact researchers in self-determination theory, a macro-theory of basic human psychological needs. I commissioned a more in-depth study on the physiology of creative storytelling, funded by a presidential grant, and we refined the premise: Decision-making is a survival tool. Therefore, decision outcomes should lead to the satisfaction of physical and psychological needs. If the context and need are understood, then the decision outcome is predictable. Context, need, outcome — know any two, derive the third. The study conclusion agreed that although the premise was simple, the math was still hard. A more robust data-mining tool would be required.

I made some calls to contacts in Silicon Valley and proposed an international public-private technology demonstration to military leadership. I advocated Southeast Asia as the appropriate locale for a field test, knowing that the State Department would prioritize the region to counterbalance Chinese influence. Embassy support came easy. Joint Staff leadership, however, wanted to limit my budget.

I stood before a familiar face to argue my case.

"You want how much, PB?" yelled the Vice Chairman of the Joint Chiefs of Staff, who happened to be the former Vice Chief of Naval Operations. When it came to taxpayer dollars, the vice could be quite the screamer.

I waited a couple of beats. "Thirty days of operating funds that will be applied to all Navy assets. The State Department will cover their own costs. Silicon Valley's share will be gratis. The tech companies have some cutting-edge tools they'd like to show off."

"Of course, they do," he gruffed. "They know the game. Today's goodwill is tomorrow's noncompetitive, long-term contract." The vice chair looked over my proposal papers. "Looks like you did your homework. Rising China. Waning interest in the Middle East. We are done in Iraq. You're lucky too, PB."

"How so, sir?"

"The Joint Chiefs want to lean our national defense strategy toward the Pacific Theater. The president is on board." He rifled through other papers scattered on his desk. "But don't construe a presidential blessing with unlimited funding." He paused and swiveled his chair toward the window and looked out toward Arlington Cemetery. "Ten days will get you started. If the technology is as good as you say, and you find our boys with it...well...that would be a game changer. Keep the thirty-day plan in reserve and send me daily updates. This mission will likely have White House-level attention, and I don't want the chairman blindsided if it's not working."

I chose not to respond.

He stood and walked to the window. "Answer me this question: Why are you doing this? Most of my terminal flag officers check out after a year. What's in it for you? Some personal connection I don't know about?"

"I *do* know a family who is living through the pain of a missing son." I stopped myself from adding any more detail. "And I'm a helicopter pilot. Rescue is what we do."

He smiled and walked back to his desk. "Fair enough." As he signed the funding approval form, he closed the conversation. "Get yourself a good team, PB. And bring our boys home."

As I walked the Pentagon corridors toward the Metro, I contemplated the vice chairman's question. "Why *was* I doing this?" Throughout the mission-planning process, I had been careful to de-emphasize any singular pursuit of Michael as a priority—though I had assigned myself as the case officer to his family. In my pursuit of mission data and soldier narratives, I had gleaned much of Michael's backstory. I knew far more about Michael than I had revealed.

He was a good big brother. Lori had made that clear in her letters, emails, Facebook posts, and Instagram stories. She always used the present tense when referring to Michael. She spoke of his uplifting spirit but longed for his physical presence to punctuate his memory. For Lori, memories of Michael inspired and pushed her to great success. His comfort and comedy softened the pain she felt as a child allegedly born by mistake. Thinking about his absence and the circumstances surrounding his disappearance would drive her into a deep depression, dragging her down to her lowest depths. She missed his masculine presence, which compensated for a distant and preoccupied father in her youth. In Lori's mind, Michael was not dead, though her parents had given him up long before. She was adamant: "If he is missing, he cannot be dead."

He was a good friend. While Lori galloped the globe in the Foreign Service, Patty stayed at Woodland Hill. She rose through the faculty ranks, volunteering to be the school's first interim principal when Woodland Hill Elementary transitioned to Myers Charter. Interim soon became permanent. Michael would be proud of her and what she had achieved throughout her many years as an educator. She stood up for children as Michael stood up for her in the 1970s. While Patty searched for her identity and came to terms with her sexual orientation, Michael protected her from social bias and adolescent immaturity. "He made me strong," she said.

As the family's representative, Patty frequently met me at the National Archives to pore over raw battlefield after-action reports from Vietnam. We researched transcripts, maps, logbooks, and taped recollections from aging veterans for clues of his whereabouts. Patty was dedicated to his cause: "We were more than brother and sister one year apart. We were best friends. I miss him so much. I want to bring him home."

He was a good son. Visiting Patch at the veterans assisted-living facility gave me yet another perspective of Michael—that of his parent. Patch lacked short-term cognitive recall but still had plenty of distant memories of Michael. I provided him updates on the project status and pumped him for information about Michael's motivations, behavioral tendencies, and decision-making capability.

His recall often strayed to his 1950 combat experience—fighting in freezing temperatures against Chinese communist forces who had just invaded the southern portion of the Korean peninsula. Patch's 1st Marine Division had suffered heavy losses. There had never been a full accounting for many of his comrades. Rather than dwell on tragedy, Patch befriended the families of the missing. His nights at the local Veterans of Foreign War post detracted from his "home guard" responsibilities, but he made no apologies. Michael learned from his father's example — he gave attention to those who needed it most.

He was a catcher. Michael's boyhood love of baseball was well known. He played catcher, like me. Catchers are the type of people who want to control situations and be in on every play. He likely thrived on taking charge but would never call out a teammate. He built up others or covered for their mistakes. He was a hustler, letting the dirt on his uniform speak to his commitment. He was a leader.

He loved the outdoors. Michael wasn't quite a tree-hugger, as Patch would say, but he was an explorer fascinated by nature, especially animals. Patty confirmed as much. Patch would take her and Michael camping often. Lori was deemed too young for the rigor of her siblings' adventures, so she stayed home with her mom. While camping, Michael wandered off on more than a few occasions, getting lost in the woods. And he always returned. Patch said, "I just had to wait. I never went out searching for him. He always found his way back."

Our analytical profile of Michael supported much of what I already suspected. His lean-forward approach to life and his loyalty to teammates drove his decision-making.

Michael started his tour in Vietnam in a rear-guard mechanized unit, a random but not uncommon in-country placement for newcomers. Factual data — recollections and paperwork — placed him in Da Nang in early 1972. The absence of information later that spring raised the possibility of reassignment. There were multiple covert operations to which he could have volunteered, and the paperwork trail would be thin.

Combat rescue was one such opportunity that fit Michael's personality. The CIA recruited door gunners and rescue aircrew from Da Nang for assignment in countries that bordered Vietnam. Following the combat-rescue thread, we asked the computer where a hard-charging, risk-taking, nature-oriented young Army soldier would find himself in the spring of 1972. The answer was Laos. Not only for Michael but for over three hundred soldiers like him. All missing, all their families tagged with the Gold Star.

With the vice chairman's endorsement, I recruited my team of experts. State Department global special envoys had proliferated after the September 11 terrorist attacks. A special envoy is a diplomatic expert, ambassadorial in everything but the title. They provide a laser focus on political issues that transcend international boundaries. In 2015, Lori was a deputy special envoy for North Korean human rights issues in Seoul—a top-level job on the embassy team. She was highly regarded in the Foreign Service, hoping one day to become a full ambassador. I sought Lori's help with navigating interagency processes and opening a diplomatic channel to the Laotian military.

My small analytic team had grown into a task force. Lori expertly negotiated the strict security protocols that would allow me to bring highly secret and very expensive spy technology into a communist country. Since I did not possess the deft political magic needed to walk battlefield terrain with a former enemy, I requested a State Department liaison from the US embassy. I should not have been surprised that after flying Stacey to Seoul to watch Charlie, Lori flew to Vientiane. She had detailed herself to my team.

9

2015
Mission Day 1
Vientiane, Laos

In the spring of 2015, members of the US-Laos Joint Task Force for Personnel Recovery assembled in Vientiane, the capital of the Lao People's Democratic Republic. I arrived with a small administrative staff and a flight crew—pilots and mission specialists—aboard an NP-3D Orion turboprop on loan from the Navy. The Orion was configured with an array of high-tech sensors and data processors.

Lori arrived with Noy, a Lao linguist and biodiversity expert from the Greater Mekong World Wildlife Fund. Lori had recruited Noy for her extensive knowledge of the Xe Sap National Protected Area, the geographic focal point of our search.

The night before our official mission kickoff, I sent the team members into the city to bond but asked Lori to stay behind and dine with me at the hotel. My excuse was to brief her on executive-level mission details, but my real reason was to check her emotional state.

"Are you ready for this?" I asked.

"Ready for what?"

"For what we may find in the next few days."

"You mean *who* we may find?"

I nodded. "The Laotian government is permitting us to fly on scripted routes in the northeast quadrant of Sekong Province. The Orion has a canopy-penetrating camera that we'll employ over a portion of Xe Sap. The terrain is masked from normal radar by mountains. The area is heavily forested and only lightly touched by development. It's a decent location for a rescue helicopter to fly a holding pattern just above the trees."

"You're a rescue pilot. You would know. But are you sure Michael was on a helicopter?"

"I had a case officer go through the CIA archives. We confirmed that Michael got himself detailed to operations here in 1972. He volunteered to be a gunner and a rescue crewman on a Jolly Green Giant helicopter. Jolly Greens operated out of secret bases here in Laos to support covert bombing missions. US strategy that year was to disrupt North Vietnamese arms and supply shipments on the Laotian side of the South Vietnam border. If a fighter jet or bomber aircraft was disabled from anti-aircraft fire, Xe Sap was considered a safe area for pilots to bail out or egress to."

Lori nodded. "That sounds like Michael. He would've taken a tough outdoor mission if it was available. In a few letters, he complained about his desk job in Da Nang. Mom read his letters to me at breakfast before school. But the letters stopped in the spring of 1972. I remember that time so well. That was when we started to fall apart." She halted the story as the waiter brought our first course— *tum mak hoong*, a papaya salad.

I thanked the waiter and steered the conversation back to the present, choosing my words carefully. "Our working theory is that

Michael's Jolly Green was on a rapid response mission and may have gone down while in a holding pattern in the eastern mountains of Xe Sap. We know from logs that they launched. There is no record of any fixed-wing needing rescue. But airborne holding was a common practice."

"Was he shot down?"

"The Xe Sap mountains are steep, and the navigation technology wasn't great back then. Pilot error might have been a factor. For this recovery mission, it doesn't matter. My team and I think the trees are hiding a crash site."

I paused to let the statement sink in. Lori didn't say anything, so I continued. "The plan is to fly the Orion the day after tomorrow. The scripted routes will include areas of interest to the Lao government. We can view the unclassified raw data in the airplane and transmit photo data to the Naval Research Lab in Anacostia, Virginia, using a satellite uplink. Lab personnel are standing by to receive and process the information against our secure database.

"Xe Sap's topography is challenging. The foliage is thick, but the canopy-piercing camera uses laser-ranging technology. The engineers have been tinkering with an optical process that can see behind trees and discern old-growth from new-growth forests. The system is sensitive enough to detect anomalies of a certain size and even spike an alert to an exposed piece of metal or other aircraft debris."

"Can it detect human remains?"

"It's not that sensitive. But a separate team of contractors will be joining us tomorrow to field test a drone with some unique capabilities. It can integrate an array of sensors in real time with proprietary and national databases. They claim they can pinpoint exact locations for us to infiltrate. Less time on the search, more time on repatriation. That's how I sold my boss on paying for this mission." I took a sip of wine and steered the conversation toward mission planning details.

"Once we use the Orion to narrow the search area, the Laotian Air Force has agreed to stage us in the nearest village to continue a localized search. Two Laotian helicopter crews, a linguist, and an ordnance expert will join our team.

"The Laotian government is keen on ridding the countryside of unexploded ordnance, and my contractor claims the drone can sort out bomb locations, too. That was a key selling point for host-country approval. The Laotian countryside is littered with submunitions from cluster bombs dropped in the late 60s and early 70s. If this mission goes as planned, we will have a diplomatic tool that can help find more missing personnel and bring them home. There are over three hundred American service members still missing in Laos."

"Is your goal to find *them* — or Michael?"

"I know more about Michael's case than all the others. This is a feasibility exercise. A prototype strategy. I must take my chances with what I know. We have a limited amount of time and a finite budget so *my* goal is to find Michael and his seven crewmates."

"I appreciate that, Peter," she said. "And I love you for what you are doing. But are you doing this for *me*? There are seven American families like mine who will benefit from this mission. To the contrary, there are another three hundred families that would rather you focus on *their* sons and brothers. Add another three thousand Laotian families who could use our help. Where is the line between professional and personal interests? I don't want you to play favorites."

Her words shook me. Like many of our past conversations,

our intimate discussion was bending toward a global cause and an ethical dilemma. Is this the conversation that two superheroes have the night before they fly off to save the world? In trying to fix one problem, we discover a hundred more to solve? Sorting personal and professional motivations was not a strong suit for either of us.

I fell back to a baseball metaphor. "Let's play the game one pitch at a time. The mission planning brief is tomorrow. The next day, we fly. There's a monsoon off the coast of Vietnam, so one day of flying time may be all we get. Weather will be a factor, but we have the perfect team for this mission. I believe in them.

"Still, there's a risk that whatever we find regarding the crew of the Jolly Green will be inconclusive. Any physical evidence we find must be preserved and analyzed at the forensic lab in Hawai'i. Unless we find a dog tag or a marked piece of clothing, we won't be sure who it is we found."

"Do you have a field DNA kit?"

"Yes."

"And I'm here, so you have *my* DNA, right?"

I didn't answer. She stayed quiet for a while. I knew that look. She was processing. Calculating. Running through scenarios in her mind. I broke the silence after her familiar dimple appeared. She had finished her calculation.

"You don't have to go into the field," I said. "Your diplomatic magic got us into the country. You can track our progress on radio from the embassy."

She sipped her wine. "I'm going."

"We may find nothing."

"I'm going."

"We may find something."

"We may find Michael. I'm going."

"I'll ask again, are you ready for what we may find?"

She frowned. "Stop patronizing me, Peter. You said you need a diplomat on the ground. You may end up in an unfriendly village. This country is still suffering consequences from an ill-advised war some forty years ago. It's unclear to me how you will be received and whether you can handle it. I did my homework. The villagers don't trust the government. And poaching is a big problem in the protected area. You are not walking into an American national park. And I'm not some white-collar office dweller who's never seen war. I have been living with war my whole life. I'm ready for this moment.

"I deployed to the Tamil region of Sri Lanka in the middle of a civil war. I drank tea with victims of Taliban abuse in Farah. I negotiated a hostage release with a ten-year old Nigerian child soldier. That's Charlie's age, for Christ's sake. I'm ready — for whatever we may find."

She stared at me. "Are *you* ready?" she said.

"Ready for what?"

"To end this quest for Michael?"

"Of course, I am. It's my job. It's the mission. Why do you ask?"

"Because I'm scared. I'm scared about the end of *our* joint mission — yours and mine. I'm scared that if we find Michael, we will have one less bond in our relationship."

"We co-parent a son. Our bond will last for generations."

At that, her stoicism caved. I had pulled the Charlie card. She used her napkin to wipe tears.

"You won't get airsick on me tomorrow, will you?" I asked.

She threw a cherry tomato at me from her plate. Like a fastball painting the high inside corner, I caught it, nonchalantly placed it in my salad, and stared down at the Laotian first course, trying to hide the wily grin on my face.

"Are you impressed with yourself?" she asked.

I looked up. Her dimple's second appearance of the night was evidence that there was still a spark. I had not been looking for it, but it was there. We were back to intimate, but my moral compass pointed true north toward Leslie and Katya. I changed the subject.

"Can I impress you with some information?"

"You always impress me. What is it?"

"The contractor I mentioned? It's my brother Jason."

She beamed. "Now I *know* we are going to find Michael."

10

Mission Day 2
Vientiane, Laos

Commercial fixed-wing aviation is not my area of expertise, but I admit I had a flush of pilot envy as a sleek, ice-blue HondaJet approached the military ramp at Wattay International. After the jet was chocked and the engine shut down, the pilot looked our way. I saw Jason's infectious smile—he'd inherited it from Mom. Gold Ray-Ban aviator sunglasses masked Dad's contribution to my little brother's handsomeness.

I stood with Lori at the hangar's edge while my Laotian Air Force handler, Colonel Kham, checked the crew's paperwork and collected their passports as they exited the jet. Lori leaned over. "Is Jason still single?" she whispered.

"You're quite the cougar today," I mumbled.

"Well, you are falling in love with his private jet. What do you call that?"

"Retirement," I said.

Colonel Kham waved to me. I deferred to Lori to lead our entourage toward Jason and his crew, meeting them halfway on the blistering hot tarmac. Hugs and handshakes were subdued as everyone played their best diplomatic partner-nation-building role to perfection. Colonel Kham guided us all to a conference room, where a small gathering of photographers and news reporters had assembled in one corner. Friendship, collaborative problem-solving, and a future built on trust and dialogue were themes offered to the pool, first by the colonel at the head of the table and then by me, sitting to his right. My demeanor probably came off flat. But I was smart enough to allow the final word to come from Lori, whom I introduced as the soul of the mission. She stood and walked toward the press gaggle.

"*Sabaideebor,*" she said, greeting the assembly in a perfect Lao dialect. She owned the room as she placed her hands together at her mouth and performed the customary short bow known as a *nop*. "There will soon come a day when brothers do not fight, when sisters do not weep for their lost brothers. There will soon come a day when mothers and fathers will smile because their children are not fighting, and the search for the lost brother can begin. When that day comes, each of us must ask ourselves, 'Did I do enough to find the brother who was lost?'" She glanced around the room.

"Today, this small, powerful team from two countries — whose only previous bond was war — will work together and do their best in the cause of finding our brothers and returning them home to their mothers and fathers. We dearly want the mothers and fathers to smile again and the sisters to weep no more. I am honored to be on this team, representing all the weeping sisters of war. Bless us as we try to do our best." Lori widened her arms to embrace the atmosphere as cameras clicked. "*Khob chai,*" she said, again in perfect Lao dialect, as microphones lunged at her and the room buzzed in two languages.

Colonel Kham directed his staff to escort the press out. He then introduced me and relinquished control of the room as I presided over briefings for the next three hours. I adjourned the session after a comprehensive review of the mission and a deep dive into the tactical plan and its contingencies. And after watching Jason's eyelids succumb to gravity.

Lori and I, by virtue of our rank and diplomatic status, had a sedan and a military escort waiting to take us back to the hotel. A bus would take the rest of the team. Though he protested, Jason, by virtue of his relationship to me, would ride in the sedan with us.

"I want to ride in one of those *tuk tuks*," he said referring to the ornately decorated half-motorcycle, half-rickshaw taxis that were poised just outside the airport boundary. Kham looked at me.

"He's kidding," I said, though I knew my brother was serious.

Chez, a member of Jason's crew, rolled a hard-case travel bag to him. "Don't forget your toys, Jason."

"Thanks, Chez. I have to ride with the grown-ups for now, but I'll be back with the crew in no time. Will you gas up Mabel and get her ready to go for tomorrow?"

His crew member smiled, gave a subtle wink, then walked back to the flight line.

Lori looked perplexed. "His jet has a name," I said.

Jason allowed the sedan driver to place the case in the trunk only after he cautioned him on its fragility. "Be gentle with Clara. She's still a prototype." The sedan driver, who did not speak English, politely smiled and threw the hard case in the trunk. Jason grimaced. "A very expensive prototype."

I glanced at Lori. "His drone has a name, too."

Lori demanded the middle of the back seat, though Jason offered to take it. She reasoned that she had to keep "the boys" from fighting.

While the driver and Kham talked in Lao, the three of us shed our rank and stature. We were kids again. It was a matter of milliseconds before Lori accosted Jason. "When did you get a jet? And when did you learn to fly?"

"I didn't. And I haven't. Chez is a pilot. But she didn't fly the airplane here—the airplane flew itself. Autonomous control. I wrote the program for it. So, I guess in some way, since the plane taught itself to fly, that makes me the pilot, right?" Jason beamed as he started to brag about the intricacies of machine-learned autonomous flight control. "I wish it were *my* jet," he said. "Chez is the chief test pilot at our Japanese affiliate. Generally, I don't like test pilots, but she's an exception."

"That's enough out of you, Buzz Lightyear," I said.

"You can call me Chief Technology Officer. Some people even call me Senior Vice President for Technology Development."

"I'll always call you *little* brother."

Lori grabbed a hand from both of us and squeezed them tight as the car arrived at the hotel valet entrance. I guessed by her smile what she was thinking.

We are going to find Michael.

11

Mission Day 3
Xe Sap National Protected Area, Laos

To say that the Orion's cabin area did not have the new carpet smell of Mabel—Jason's corporate robot jet—would be quite the understatement.

Instead of windows to view the scenery, there were four portals meant for a 1980s crew looking for Cold War submarines. These tiny, bubbled windows hardly offered enough lighting to offset the cabin's claustrophobic gloom. Adding to the discomfort was an air-conditioning system that put out a near-constant blast of cold fog to keep the massive internal electronics cool. Anyone aboard who had a flight jacket wore it over their task force-branded flight suits. I let Lori borrow mine.

One attribute the Orion shared with Mabel was a barf bag, and I needed it about an hour into the flight. From the moment we took off, my control of the mission morphed into oversight and my anxiety transitioned from a simple ocular migraine to gut-wrenching abdominal pain. The crew chief was astute enough to recognize that I was airsick. He escorted me to the aft-station bunk area under the pretense of having me review a terrain map on his electronic tablet.

Closing the curtain, he left me alone to hurl the full contents of my breakfast. He then directed me to a bunk, where I laid long enough to clear my head, catch my breath, and allow my stomach to calm. When I finally emerged from behind the curtain, I accepted a bottled water from the crew chief. Patting his shoulder, I offered unspoken gratitude for his discretion and returned to my jump seat.

We had arrived over the eastern sector of Xe Sap, and the optical technology had been employed. Sensor operators, ears cupped with old-school plug-in push-button headsets, were homed in on flat-screen displays and scopes, exchanging professional chatter with each other and with the cockpit mission commander. Each member of the Navy research team was paired with a guest—either Lori's small team of two or Colonel Kham's Lao liaisons. From my jump-seat vantage point, I watched everyone like a catcher watches his fielders handling a ball in play.

The crew chief returned with a cup of coffee from the galley. Bypassing the intercom system, he shouted over the hum of the engines and the blast of the air conditioner. "Ms. Lori said you could use this."

I thanked him and glanced toward the front. Lori was at the most-forward camera workstation, fully engaged with Josey, my lead analyst. The two pored over the holographic images streaming their way to the console's plasma screen.

I found myself staring at Lori's hair, which took me back to sixth grade. It still curled to the middle of her back like wet spaghetti—all twisted and curvy. The reds were not as dark anymore, and the golden brown speckles were not so dominant, but the essence of cinnamon stuck in my mind.

She turned and flashed a dimpled smile. I raised my cup to

acknowledge her thoughtfulness. Josey looked particularly excited by her screen and waved me forward. I left my headset on the jump seat and proceeded to their station. I shouted over the aircraft noise. "Got something, Josey?"

"Admiral," she said, "this pass is showing some concentrated deforestation similar to our test profiles." She pointed to a three-dimensional terrain grid that distinguished relative canopy thickness using color and referred to a small area that appeared orange in a sector that was otherwise intensely green. "It may indicate a village clearing or a site that was selectively bombed, but the small acreage is more aligned with what we are looking for." Josey looked at Lori, concerned with the appropriate choice of words.

Lori put her at ease. "Could it be a crash site?"

Josey nodded, but referred to the screen. "It fits the profile we trained on."

"Good work, Josey," I praised. "It's a good piece of data, but there might be more. I can't change the flight path without sacrificing data from the rest of the sector. We have a lot more area to cover with the camera. Has the data link with Anacostia been established?"

"Locked on and streaming," Josey said.

"Let's stick with the plan, but go ahead and brief the team on your findings." I turned to the crew chief, who joined me at my side. "Can you get some corroborating sensors on these high-interest areas?"

"Already coordinating, sir. Station two is blasting anti-tank radar. A Jolly Green would give a good return if she went down intact."

Since I wasn't on the headset, I wasn't clued in on the coordination that was already occurring around the camera data. I was not offended to be the last one to know what was going on. I had worked with admirals who gummed up tactical decision-making in situations like these by receding into lieutenant-like behavior. My time aboard this flight was best spent cheerleading and encouraging the team. As for the overall mission, there were real-world concerns outside the skin of the Orion that were singularly my responsibility. Though the vice chairman had acted as my ally in the proposal stage, I feared that any hint of project weakness or underperformance would be an excuse for him to redirect our project funding to a more glamorous warfighting need. I took the POW/MIA slogan, "You are not forgotten," and added my own corollary: "but we are not fully funded to find you."

I had another anxious concern—that of technology transfer. I had invited host-nation liaison officers—from a communist nation, at that—to join us in a Navy patrol airplane stuffed with sophisticated, highly-sensitive technology. Information needed to be cautiously shared with Colonel Kham and his crew, lest it make its way to the Lao northern border and into the hands of the other "people's republic." Though I trusted the colonel as a soldier, pilot, and leader, we were from different teams, and our current alliance was not guaranteed to last beyond personnel recovery or unexploded ordnance removal.

There was also a chance that we would come up empty—that all our technology and the huge, classified data-mining investment project I had started back at the Naval Research Lab would find nothing but a discarded tractor at a long-forgotten logging camp. This probability fueled my greatest fear—that of disappointing Lori and not keeping the promise I made to her so many years ago.

I asked Noy, Lori's Wildlife Fund expert, to join me in the aft cabin galley to talk over the results, and Lori followed. We plugged our headsets into the galley intercom ports and selected a private channel.

"Noy, the team is getting pretty excited about the data flowing in from the canopy-penetrating camera, but I'm worried about false positives. You were on the crew that just concluded a biodiversity survey of the area. Based on your knowledge of the Xe Sap terrain, how reliable are the data we are getting? What else could cause these contrasts between old-growth and new-growth forests?"

Noy started talking but forgot to press the intercom button. Lori helped her figure it out. "Sorry about that, Admiral," she said. She took a deep breath to calm her nerves, then spoke with authority. "I believe the team should temper its excitement about the data because poachers and loggers have operated in the protected areas for many years. The new growth may in fact be remnants of abandoned encampments. We are off to a good start, but I believe we should compare today's data with the terrain maps we marked up from our field study. I can recruit my old survey crew to help. They should be reachable by phone, if not in person. It was a small staff, though, and there's lots of data to review in a very short time."

"I can help you," Lori said. "My aide and I will come to your office. I can probably get some embassy staff to assist."

"I'm sure Jason would also like to help," I said. "The map study will help his team get a jump on where to deploy Clara."

When Noy looked confused, Lori explained about Jason's propensity for naming his technology. Noy giggled and leaned over to whisper to Lori without pressing the intercom button, but I read her lips. "He's the cute one, right?"

Before I could think of a clever quip, the crew chief stuck his head into the galley. His face was unsmiling and sober. "Sir, your presence is requested in the cockpit." He pointed to his electronic tablet that displayed weather radar. As if on cue, the plane shimmied in a pocket of turbulence.

I shuffled forward—past the subdued blue light of the workstation flat-screens, through the dense fog pouring from the air conditioner, and up to the cockpit door. As I entered, I had to brace myself as the plane turned west, now diverting from the preplanned north-south flight route. The flight engineer offered me his center seat, and I plugged in my headset to hear the cockpit discussion.

I knew what was coming but let the lieutenant commander pilot tell me first. "Admiral, the mountains are generating some weather effects. I can get closer to the Vietnamese border, but the turbulence would be hell for the crew." This was his diplomatic way of saying it was time to return to Wattay.

I looked over to Kham in the observer seat, who concurred. "It does not get better, Admiral. I believe these gentlemen are great pilots, and I thank them for the privilege to ride in the cockpit, but these mountains have a way of speaking to you. I believe what they are saying."

I turned to face the mission commander, an officer I had known for many years. He nodded his head. "I surveyed all the flight stations and sensor operators, sir. They report good canopy penetration for eighty percent of the objective terrain. Multiple radar hits also. Anacostia reports a good link. They have what they need for the database merge. Our test objectives have been met, sir. My call is to terminate and return to base, but I am subject to your orders as the senior flag officer. Your concurrence is requested to terminate the mission…sir." The pause made clear his preferred course of action.

I knew the rules, and so did he. As an unrestricted line admiral, I could take full command of the aircraft and direct the pilots to continue to fly into storms in the name of mission accomplishment — ironically, the very decision the helicopter aircraft commander of Michael's Jolly Green likely made in the spring of 1972. Should they have flown regardless of weather in the name of a rescue that may — or may not — have been needed? Or should they have abandoned their holding pattern and aborted the mission, sparing their own crew?

"Return to base," I ordered and left the cockpit.

12

Mission Day 4
Vientiane, Laos

I grounded the flight mission for weather on day four. The monsoon off the southern coast of Vietnam had stagnated, and its outer bands of wind and rain lay atop the Xe Sap border region I most wanted to scan. The weather in Vientiane, however, was a perfect Southeast-Asian tropical day. Except for lunch with the US ambassador and the Laotian Minister of Foreign Affairs, I spent the working hours at the embassy, consumed by the "what ifs" of Mission Michael's field test. What if we found nothing? What if the technology broke? What if we found something unexpected — like a mass gravesite? Or found more than we ever expected, like fields of unexploded ordnance?

Every question had an answer, a response, and a coordinated action plan. The most complex plan — by the sheer number of assets required — would be initiating the Department of Defense's process of repatriating American service members, the procedures of which are well practiced. Site excavation and recovery are manpower intense. Add to that host-nation protocols and any religious accommodations required for a dignified transfer. Were we to discover a crash site with human remains, a C-17 Globemaster would launch from Joint Base

Pearl Harbor, Hawai'i, arriving in less than twenty-four hours with recovery and identification experts from my home agency.

Over lunch, the ambassador, minister, and I had discussed these arrangements and all the branches and sequels to our current plan of action. Adding to my stress was the US ambassador's mention of a potential visit to Laos from the American secretary of state. A Vietnam War veteran himself, the secretary had prioritized Pacific Rim and Southeast Asian nations for diplomatic engagement. The trip, scheduled for later that year, was contingent upon the results of our new technological approach to finding missing personnel. Such a visit by the secretary was usually a precursor to a subsequent stopover from the President of the United States. Oversight and interest from the entire chain of command wouldn't normally bother me, but I admit I didn't eat much at lunch and spent the better part of the afternoon on the phone, confirming details of the larger second phase of the mission.

To get my mind off work, I called Charlie, who was in the care of Stacey, Patty's fiancée, while Lori was in Laos. "How are you, buddy?" I opened with a classic disarming question.

"Good."

"What are you doing?"

"Nothing."

I heard a video game in the background. "Are you having fun with Auntie Stacey?"

"Yeah."

"Did you have baseball practice yesterday?"

"Yup."

"How'd that go?"

"Good."

I sensed he was tired of talking to me. "Well, I miss you, buddy."
Silence.

"I think Momma will call you later. She's at work right now."

"Okay."

"I'll say goodbye for now. Can you give the phone to Auntie
Stacey?" I threw in, "I love you, Charlie," but I was pretty sure that
the phone was already being handed off.

"He heard you, Peter." Stacey was now on the other end. "Are
we close to finding Michael?" she asked.

"I'll know in an hour or two. Lori and Jason are at the Wildlife
Fund headquarters, poring over terrain maps and interviewing field
researchers who may have clues of a helicopter crash site. All the
technology I brought to this mission has only added to the confusion.
There are five or six potential areas I want to look at, but the budget is
limited, and I have to prioritize one, maybe two over the others. I'm
inclined to order a search in whatever location Lori recommends."

"That's a smart move, Peter. I can't explain it, but that family has
a sixth sense about Michael. He seems to be calling them with some
sort of cosmic voice. I can tell that this quest is bringing Patty, Lori,
and Patch closer together. Closer than I have ever seen them."

I did not respond. If the family's hopes hinged on me, I feared
their disappointment.

"How are you holding up, Peter?" asked Stacey.

"I'm good," I said, thankful that she couldn't see my eyes
through the telephone.

"Yeah, right," she said.

I cleared my throat and wiped my eyes. "We are so close

to finding Michael, Stacey. I know we are. But I'm running out of time, and the project is running out of money. I could do without the bureaucratic headaches and the nagging oversight. Sometimes, I wish I had retired earlier. I need to go home. I need to pay attention to Charlie and Katya before they grow up. And I need to recharge my marriage with Leslie.

"I've been chasing Michael's ghost for ages. If we don't find him on this trip, Lori, Patty, Patch…they'll be devastated. I think I'm at the limit of how I can help."

The therapist appeared. "So why do you keep chasing him? Why did you defer retirement and sacrifice your life to find a boy you barely knew who went missing so long ago?"

I choked up again. "Because my shipmates would have done it for me. And it's a promise our country has made, to leave no soldier behind. It's my job to keep that promise."

"I think it's something more than that, Peter. You don't have to say it out loud, but at least say it to yourself." Stacey was right. And I didn't say it out loud.

I had constructed an elaborate, highly expensive technical enterprise to serve my personal desires, rationalizing every decision as being aligned with national interests. I skirted every rule in the acquisition guidebook under the guise of "prototype." I made a technological alliance with a blood relative. I waved a presidential decision memorandum at every admiral and general who threatened to challenge my funding line, not caring what any peer would think of me in an obscure and uncertain post-retirement future. I thought I cared for all three hundred families of the missing. But did I really? Was I chasing Michael's ghost? Or was I chasing Lori?

"I have to go now," I said. "Will you call Patty and let her know our status? I promised the other families an update also, so tell her to keep the mission details under wraps until I draft an official statement."

"Before you do that, Peter, I have a suggestion."

"I'm listening."

"Call Leslie."

Later in the evening, while I was drafting a status report for the chain of command, the ambassador's adjutant alerted me to the arrival of a motorcade. I went to the entrance to greet my team, whom I assumed completed their work at the Wildlife Fund headquarters. Colonel Kham stepped out of a sedan and offered a brisk salute—a signal of respect not required by international norms but very much appreciated.

"Admiral, the Royal Lao Air Force is at your disposal and ready for our next mission phase tomorrow. We will take a transport to our base in Pakse. From there, with your permission, we will helicopter our team to the village of Ta Vang. The distinguished lady and your brother believe they have the proper coordinates for your search near the village. It would be my honor to fly you there."

"Very well, Colonel. May I ask where the distinguished lady and my not-so-distinguished brother are?"

"They will be arriving shortly by tuk tuk," he said, smiling. "Your brother insisted. I will not be surprised if he gives the tuk tuk a name."

13

Mission Day 5
Ta Vang, Laos

The flight south from Vientiane to Pakse was aboard a Soviet-era transport plane that left me pining for the NP-3D Orion except for its bubble windows—the view of the grand Mekong River on final approach was stunning. I had whittled our team down to seven essential personnel. Chez would double as Jason's technician and babysitter. Noy was cast as our linguistic expert, as she had some familiarity with the indigenous dialects we would encounter at the remote village. Two Navy special-warfare chief petty officers were detailed for this phase of the mission. Chief Moore was a specialist in tactical jungle operations, and Chief Favors brought ordnance identification and de-arming expertise to our US contingent. At Lori's suggestion, I dispensed with the requirement for uniforms so as to not intimidate any locals whose help we might need. We were prepared to spend up to three days in the field. Because each member of the team was responsible for their own attire, the chiefs looked cut from a survivalist magazine while the rest of us looked more like models from an L.L. Bean catalog.

Upon landing at Pakse International, we were whisked by airport officials to two UH-1H "Huey" helicopters, their rotors turning at idle. A crewman pointed me to Colonel Kham's chopper, where I took the left seat in the cockpit. Donning a headset, I was greeted by a bright smile. "Admiral, do you still remember how to fly this aircraft?"

I finished strapping my five-point harness and clicked the microphone switch on the center cyclic control. "I haven't flown a Huey since flight school, but the cockpit looks very familiar. I think I can handle it." I gripped the collective/throttle with my left hand, held the center cyclic steady with my right, and stretched my legs to reach the yaw pedals on the floor.

"Then it is my honor to give you the controls." Kham showed his hands, indicating a positive transfer of control of the aircraft.

"I have the aircraft," I acknowledged. I was now the pilot of a helicopter for the first time in ten years—and a Royal Lao Air Force one at that. I turned my head to see who else was in my aircraft. Chez, Favors, and Noy filled the backseats along with the Laotian crew chief and a backup pilot. Lori, Jason, and Moore jumped into the backseat of the second Huey. With our gear and Clara—our most valuable piece of equipment—strapped down and secured, the crew chief signaled his readiness. Kham handled all the radio calls in perfect English, and we lifted off.

A saying among helicopter pilots is that we are at our best flying "IFR." A fixed-wing fighter would interpret this acronym to mean "instrument flight rules." But to a helicopter pilot, IFR means "I follow roads." And that's what I did for the first half of the one-hour flight. We flew the formation five hundred feet above ground level at the pedestrian pace of ninety knots. I banked and weaved my lead Huey as smoothly as possible in consideration for my wingman, who was in loose formation to my right. The weather was CAVU, aviation-speak for ceiling and visibility unlimited. Past the city of Sekong, a marvelous forest appeared below. The Sekong River's meandering path led us into higher elevations. Kham programmed a set of landing zone coordinates near a field station south of Ta Vang into the tactical navigation display.

About five miles from the landing zone, I admitted to Kham that I might be rusty on the landing. He expressed his confidence in me as only a pilot could. "I don't think you will crash today." With that, I flew over the landing zone and caught sight of the windsock that defined the best angle for approach. I transitioned from flight to hover, calling upon every bit of pilot muscle memory and instinct I had. The touchdown was perfect.

THE EASTERNMOST SECTOR OF XE Sap juts into Vietnam for ninety square miles south of the 17th parallel, the historic demarcation line between the communist north and the corrupt democratic regime of the south. The Ho Chi Minh Trail—the war-era pathway North Vietnam used to transport arms and supplies—went through sovereign Laotian territory, including Xe Sap. Like a modern highway, the Ho Chi Minh Trail had exit ramps, the first of which lay north of Xe Sap. The second lay just south of its mountains. North Vietnam channeled a persistent flow of Soviet-style military support from the second off-ramp to communist fighting forces staging hit-and-run guerrilla-style tactics only forty miles from the US military beachhead at Da Nang. To disrupt the flow of arms at exit two, US air power concentrated its bombing campaigns on exit one. But Xe Sap was relatively spared of cluster bombs and deforesting napalm. Instead, the rugged hills and heavy forest cover of Xe Sap were deemed by expert planners of the day as a selected area for evasion and given the ironic acronym "SAFE."

The analytic profile projected for Michael's mission put him squarely over the SAFE terrain of Xe Sap, surrounded by hostile forces using the Ho Chi Minh Trail and villagers who woke up one day to find war on their doorstep.

The precise coordinates to start the drone search for Michael were vetted by our analytics team in Anacostia. The center of the search pattern lay a few miles away from the village of Ta Vang, near a research outpost. The facility, a repurposed mining camp, would be our base of operations for Clara's inaugural operational test flight. Kham had suggested in our mission planning brief that we should conduct drone operations away and out of sight of any village population, lest the residents think their government had nefarious intent. I thought nothing of the suggestion at the time and did not consult the team on the matter. Shortly after we shut down the helicopters, I regretted my lapse in judgment.

Kham and his crew marched a short distance to the village edge, where a few onlookers had gathered to witness the formation landing. He returned to assure us that the villagers were ready to welcome us as "eco-tourists." He did not promise them that we would stay in their accommodations, but we would be expected to spend our kip—Laotian currency—on meals and trinkets.

"Why would you tell them we are tourists?" Lori protested. "We are here to find my brother and his crew. They deserve the truth."

"My apologies, Madam Lori. But the history of this sector is complicated. It is best to ease into our purpose."

Before I said anything, Jason said, "It's not a lie. We are learning tons about the rich resources of this great nation and the importance of preserving the biodiversity in this protected area." An emerging politician, he winked at Noy, who had emphasized such points already. Then he turned to Lori, pointing to Clara's travel packs, which were resting on the shoulders of chiefs Moore and Favors. "Also, there is a lot of technology in these two backpacks. I'd rather not run a science fair out here. I'd be hard pressed to explain to the villagers what's going on with the technology without spilling some significant detail." He was playing the operational security card with me. I nodded but remained silent.

Lori's biting words, understandable as they were, had surprised everyone. She took a breath and disarmed the tension with a smile. "Thank you, Jason. And Colonel, I apologize for my abruptness. But please introduce me to the village matriarchs after you have established your connection with the leaders. I think we can learn from the women. Their perspective and knowledge will be helpful to our mission."

"Of course. The women of Ta Vang may not be the leaders in name, but I assure you that they rule the village when they must," Kham replied. He looked at Noy and spoke in his native tongue, "Did I say that right?"

Noy laughed and answered in English. "Yes, but you could have said it better."

With a sheepish grin, Kham grabbed some gear and proceeded to lead us in the direction of the mining camp. As the villagers watched the Pakse-bound Hueys take off, we hiked past their stares and smiles and marched up a moist dirt road. Kham enjoyed the company of Noy in front of the group as they spoke in Lao. Favors and Moore were fully engaged by Chez as she shared an impressive résumé of flight and travel adventures that rivaled those of the two seasoned Navy SEALS. Jason followed them, transfixed by the forest and the sounds that emanated from its darkened wall of trees. I trailed the group with Lori by my side. "Where did that challenge to our introduction as tourists come from?" I asked.

She kept her voice low. "We should be speaking the truth to the locals. The colonel is being devious. He is intent on misleading the villagers."

"He has his reasons. I believe he explained them in the pre-mission brief. He is a professional." I slowed our pace to put more distance from the group.

"This is still a communist country," said Lori. "You should be cautious about your alliance with the colonel."

"I think he is just being practical. He knows the terrain. He knows the people."

"Are you certain of that? Do you know his background? Do you know his ambition? His motivation?"

I didn't. "Kham is mission-oriented. Practical. Efficient. He knows what it takes to get the job done. He's a pilot."

"That may be enough to fly a helicopter, but our goal is to find human remains from a mission flown over forty years ago in a forest the size of Yellowstone Park. We need help. We need the local population to tell us their stories and share their memories. There may be a person or a family who can provide better information than technology. There may even be an eyewitness, perhaps someone our age, who remembers seeing or hearing something that pinpoints the location of the crew."

"This is a technology experiment, Lori. We need to find out whether the drone works. If it does, we can deploy it across the globe to find wreckage sites and missing crewmembers—for our nation as well as others. Kham knows how important this is for both our militaries."

"Don't fall back on the technology argument, Peter. You know this is about people. We need to crowdsource the search. We need local participation. And if the local population is going to help us, we must find a way to gain their trust. That's Diplomacy 101."

"We don't have the time or resources to interview all the villagers. That effort comes later. When we find clues. When we find wreckage. When we find our soldiers. Then we can piece together the narrative and understand what happened in their final hours. We can learn lessons to prevent future loss, but we must be efficient to be effective. That's Defense 101."

She huffed as the gap between our arguments matched the distance that we had fallen back from the group. "People have been around longer than your wizard toys. Human nature has a longer history than your technology."

"Physics has been around longer than people." These words came from Jason, who had sauntered back to our position, intent on nudging us along.

Beet red, Lori picked up her pace. "Whose side are you on?"

"I'm on the side of hunger," said Jason. "We are never going to make it up this hill if you two keep dragging us down. And I'm told there is food at the top of the hill."

"There's food in the village, too." Lori stormed ahead to catch up with Chez and the chiefs. I was left to walk with my brother in silence.

MY ARGUMENT WITH LORI WAS unsettling but didn't sidetrack my focus on the next phase of the mission. Dusk had fallen over the mining camp, which had been prepared for our stay by two Lao border-security guards. The food that Jason was longing for was a Lao version of a battlefield MRE, a "meal ready to eat." The khao soi — rice noodles mixed with soybeans, tomatoes, and a meat I hoped was from a hog — went over big with most of the crowd.

"Just add water," Chief Favors said, repeating the instructions on the packet.

"But first, pass it through your life-straw filtration system," Noy cautioned.

Lori claimed to have had enough MREs on deployment in Afghanistan, so she instead pressed Colonel Kham to escort her and Noy to the village, along with one of the security guards. The other guard sat at the entrance to the camp. Jason, Chez, the chiefs, and I readied Clara for her first assignment: a five-hour night reconnaissance flight. "That's how long the batteries last," Jason explained to the group.

Chief Moore, our jungle survival expert, had started a fire in a pit near the center of the compound and its modest trailers. The gas generator — our source for electrical power — provided an ambient hum that masked our conversations from the security guard, though he showed no particular interest in what we were doing anyway.

Chez unpacked Clara, unfolding her four limbs and snapping an eight-bladed rotor on each. Favors stood nearby as he listened to soft technical explanations coming from the pilot.

"Clara was light to carry," Favors said to Chez. "For me, at least. Chief Moore struggled a bit carrying his backpack up the hill."

"It's a big jungle out there, Favors," said Moore. "I'd hate to see you get lost."

Laughing, Chez took Clara apart again and handed the pieces to Favors.

"Here. Put her together yourself, just liked I showed you."

As Favors repeated the assembly, Jason spoke as if from the company brochure. "Gentlemen, Clara is simple in her design and construction, but she has a valuable component that makes her smarter than any drone in operation today." He removed his watch from his wrist and popped the backside out to reveal a microchip. He handed the chip to Chez, who gave it to Favors.

"Place this chip inside that little compartment on top," she told Favors.

Chief Moore, now curious, moved closer to observe. I had seen the demonstration but was keen to measure the SEAL's reaction to what happened next. Favors snapped the flat square from the smartwatch into a compartment on Clara's topside, causing a very dim, almost imperceptible blue light to illuminate.

"The blue light is Clara telling you she has accepted the instructions from the microchip and is ready to launch on her mission." Patting Favors on his knee, Chez said, "You did good." She turned to Moore. "It's your turn. Want to launch her?"

"You'll need my watch," Jason said. He handed the watch to Moore, who strapped it to his wrist. Moore carried Clara away from the fire pit, placed her in a shadowed clearing, and returned to sit next to Chez. She showed him which codes on the watch to press for the drone's start-up sequence.

"I can barely hear the rotors," Moore marveled.

"That's the point," Jason explained. "Quiet is good for the missions she's designed for. Are you ready to launch?"

Favors bit his lip. "Does Clara know what the mission is?"

Jason continued his sales-pitch. "I programmed her last night. A standard search pattern with options to deviate as her database fills. She'll fly on her own and come back in five hours to give us confidence levels on infiltration points. She already knows what we learned from the survey flights. I added input from our map study. Noy made some recommendations to compensate for researcher bias. Got that in the program, too. Clara is as well informed as any of us. It's time we sent her on her way. She'll create a roadmap of several excavation points and recommend how to approach them in a safe, efficient manner. She knows it's a search and rescue mission. I have other programs that can be used for hazard avoidance or even targeting."

"But we are not going to go into detail on those programs here," I interrupted. "These are discussions we can have stateside in a more secure environment." The chiefs nodded, acknowledging my concern for operational security. We were, after all, deep in the forest of a communist foreign country.

Jason looked up at the darkened sky. The fog was descending from the mountains. "Perfect time and perfect weather to fly."

Chez declared, "Time to push the launch button, jungle expert."

Moore deferred. "I'll let the bomb guy do the honors." Moore gave Chez the watch. Chez smiled and handed the watch to Favors. "She's all yours, bomb guy." She did not reveal to the chief that her fingerprint on the watch face, an additional layer of security, was necessary to initiate the passcode. She instructed Favors to press the launch button.

Favors narrated the sequence, "4-3-2-1, go!" He pressed LAUNCH. "Bye, bye Clara." The drone rose straight up into the fog with no lights and barely a whisper from the rocks and dirt that she displaced in her wake. Favors voiced his endorsement. "Admiral, we could really use one of these in the field."

"I know, Chief. I'll do my best to make sure that happens."

Jason pulled out another toy from his pack, a set of virtual-reality goggles that looked like a scuba diver mask. Favors put it on and exclaimed, "Holy ..."

Jason looked at me with the smile of a car salesman who had just nabbed a customer who paid full price. Favors was enjoying his first experience in virtual reality following the drone's flight path. We took great pleasure in watching him meander around the camp as if he were merged with Clara.

My thoughts returned to the argument with Lori and the unsatisfying MRE. "Jason, I'm going to walk to the village and check on the away team. I'll take Chief Moore with me. Can you and Chez anchor the mission while I'm gone?"

Jason, still smitten with the SEAL's endorsement of his product line, nodded his head. "Got it. I'm quite comfortable here. Chez and I will stand by in case Clara calls. But we'll also make sure Favors doesn't trip into the fire pit."

As I got up to leave, Jason stopped me. "I have something for your walk." He retrieved two items from another of his company backpacks.

I thought for a moment he was going to give us guns to ward off a tiger attack. But Noy, as part of her Wildlife Fund brief on Xe Sap, had told us that big cats were extinct in this sector — victims of a demand for tiger bones used in Chinese traditional medicine.

Jason pulled out two pairs of sunglasses and Moore and I put them on. The darkness became only darker. "Press the button on the right side," he instructed.

Once I pressed the button, the darkness brightened, and it was easy to distinguish my surroundings. "Not the best night-vision glasses I've worn," said Chief Moore, "but these will do."

Jason took the comment in business mode. "Give me a qualitative evaluation after your walk. I'll work out the bugs in an upgrade."

As we walked toward the gate, Moore whispered to me, "I was kidding. These glasses are bussin."

"Don't tell him that," I replied. "He needs to be humbled every once in a while."

Moore and I checked in with the drowsy Lao security guard, pointing toward the road to the village. The guard nodded and radioed Colonel Kham a message in Lao. We walked in silence a few hundred feet. I was lost in thought about Lori and what trouble she was brewing in the village. The chief, however, was immersed in the voices of the forest. "Do you hear them, Admiral?"

"My ears are still ringing from the helicopter. What do you hear?"

"Cicadas," he said. "The forest is alive with them." *Cicadas*, I thought. *How apropos.*

I pulled a nugget of trivia from my country study. "*Chak chan* is what they're called in the native tongue. There must be a bloom in progress. I think the cicadas in these parts have a thirteen-year cycle. All you hear are the males. They vibrate an acoustic membrane with their wings. All they want to do is get laid."

"Did you learn that in admiral school?"

"Elementary school, actually. That's where Lori and I met. We grew up together, sort of."

Moore looked at me. "I knew there was something between you two…professionally, I mean. I hope that didn't come out wrong."

"All good, Chief."

Moore chuckled as he looked around. "I'm really glad I was detailed for this mission." He was enjoying the view from the night-vision "sunglasses."

"I'm glad you are here, too," I said. "How did you learn about the assignment? I sent the request through official channels. I figured it would be denied on grounds of operational manning issues. SEALS are in such high demand."

I was pleased at Moore's explanation. "Believe me, there was some tough competition for this assignment. My dad called an old shipmate, Admiral Rasmussen, to see if I could get to the head of the line."

"You are shittin' me, sailor. Razz was my old skipper. A mentor for all my career. Same guy? Russ Rasmussen?"

"Silver Star Russ," Moore replied with a grin. "That's what my dad calls him. I just call him sir. They served in Vietnam together flying riverine patrols in the same Hueys we rode today. My dad was a Seawolf. He volunteered to be a door gunner and flew with Silver Star Russ quite a bit. Not the same mission that got him the combat rescue but enough missions to where they became friends for life."

I stopped our walk, looking Moore in the eye. "I am so glad you told me that. It's an honor to serve on this mission with you. Is your dad doing well?"

"He is, sir. Retired, of course. And I mean really retired. He does the camper thing now with my mom. Crosses the country during my deployments, looking for the best deal at a military recreation area. But he always comes back to Little Creek, Virginia, when I get home."

We started our walk again as the village lights emerged in the distance. I kept the conversation focused on him. "I surmise, Chief, that you've been deployed one too many times. Is the stress hitting you like it is the rest of the special-warfare community?"

"I'm okay, but I think there is a strain on the force. Navy SEALs, Army Rangers, Green Berets—they are all marketable. Tons of guys are cashing in. I know a few who are going to Hollywood. They see themselves as the next bachelor on that TV show. Or doing survival programs naked with some hot chick. Everything has changed in the two years since we got Bin Laden."

"Are you thinking of retiring or getting out? You know my brother, Jason, can get you a job if you need it. Most of the technology he works on is destined for the armed forces."

"Thank you, Admiral," Moore said. "I may come to that decision in a year or two. For now, I want to help Miss Lori find her brother's crew. My dad lost some close friends in the Vietnam War. I'm doing this to honor him."

We stopped talking to negotiate a particularly steep switchback in the mountain road. Then he revealed something else that I did not know. "I covered for Miss Lori in Afghanistan," he said.

"She didn't tell me that."

"I'm not sure she knows. We've been so busy getting ready for this mission, I haven't had time to talk to her. My unit shadowed her Female Engagement Team in the Farah Province of Afghanistan. Her team didn't need much cover, though. Lori's lionesses had a reputation as competent, independent, and driven. She got us the best intel, and she gained the trust of the locals better than the Army girls. She was good with a rifle, too, but her best weapon was her personality."

"We'll soon find out which weapon she's using in Ta Vang," I said. "I have a feeling there's a bar fight going on and she's in the middle of it."

"I bet she's just fine. She turned whole villages in the Farah province to our side with the way she dealt with Afghanistan's misogynistic culture. No FET I know came close to achieving what her unit did in Farah. I'm honored to cover for her on this mission. I bet her brother was quite a guy."

"I met him briefly as a boy. But I'm close to the family. Through them, I know he was — or even still is — quite the guy."

"Do you think he is still alive, Admiral?"

I slowed my steps to think about that question. "Chief, as long as I have been working POW/MIA issues, and even going back to my childhood with Lori, I've had the sense that the missing — and the departed — are always still alive in the minds of their loved ones. I know hundreds of families who remember their sons and daughters as though they never left. Their bedrooms are unchanged — same bedsheets, same trophies, toys, and knick-knacks on the shelves. Some families won't erase the messages from their kid on their answering machines. In moments of privacy, they punch the playback button to hear their soldier's voice. There is a reason that a vendor sells POW/MIA remembrance items in front of the Lincoln Memorial."

Moore chimed in. "I know the truck you're talking about. I joined a bike club and brought my hog up to the Rolling Thunder rally in D.C. I did the whole ride with them past the Wall on Memorial Day a few years back."

"So you know my answer to your question. Everyone is alive, until they're not. The data and all the evidence say that Michael and his crew are as dead as they come. But until we can confirm the circumstances of their deaths and we write the last chapter of their stories, their families will be denied the life they deserve."

The road had straightened by the time I finished talking. The village lights were bright in our night-vision view. The chief and I removed our glasses to let our unaided eyes adapt to the dim glow of the barely-lit hamlet.

Chief Moore asked a question that I think every service member asks at some point on a mission. "In Afghanistan and a few countries on this side of the planet, I was doing intel prep. Isolated operations, all by myself. Sometimes in the quiet of being deep undercover, I would ask myself, 'If I were to not return to the rendezvous point, or miss the extraction time, would somebody care? Would anybody come and get me? I know the answer is yes, but I still asked the question."

"I would come," I answered.

Moore's white teeth flashed a smile in the darkness. "I know you would. You were trained by Silver Star Rasmussen."

I pointed to the village. "Are we ready to engage the locals?"

"If this is a rescue mission to save Miss Lori, I'm in."

"I think it might be a rescue mission to save Colonel Kham," I said, a hint of a smile on my face.

As we entered the village, Chief Moore pointed out some details he'd reconnoitered from our daylight walk to the mining camp. "Most of the bamboo-walled thatched huts are family dwellings. There is an A-frame structure near the center of the village. I believe that's where they are."

"At a town hall meeting?"

"Oh, no. Remember, Favors and I are SEALS. We can smell a bar from a mile away. There is a bar behind the A-frame. I bet Miss Lori and the colonel are in there."

"Let's make a wager. Ten thousand kip says she's starting a bar fight."

Moore shook my hand. "My money is on Miss Lori. No bar fights."

We entered the village perimeter and walked straight to the A-frame, taking a narrow path to the local watering hole. "By the way," said Moore, "how much is ten thousand kip worth?"

I grinned. "About two bucks."

Through the packed room, I heard high-pitched laughter. Children always gravitated toward Lori. My intent was to stay in the background and find Colonel Kham. But a young girl grabbed me by my hand. My presence became known to all when she exclaimed, "Sailor, sailor!" She pulled me to the outer circle of adults, mostly women, who parted to reveal the inner circle of youngsters, squatting or standing as they cheered Lori and a young boy who were playing a game in the center of the room.

My little maître d' introduced me to Lori, aided in interpretation by Noy. "Khony phob phusai heu khongchao," the girl said.

"You brought me my sailor man! Good job! Khob chai!" Lori said. Noy translated. The little girl pulled me down to sit on the concrete slab floor next to Lori. "We invented a game," said Lori. "I call it Big Stick, Little Stick. I throw a big stick in the middle, then a little stick somewhere else, and my opponent, Simok, spins his top." Simok smiled at the mention of his name. "If the top stops its spinning closer to the big stick, I win. If it stops closer to the little stick, he wins." She whispered, "I've won five games in a row. This won't end until he wins."

The little girl was now sitting on my lap. She still held my left hand—my baseball glove hand. Simok looked at me, so I signaled to him as a catcher would to a pitcher, flicking my fingers twice to gain his attention. He glared at me, confused, shaking off my signal. I snuck in a smile and an obvious wink to instill in him some confidence as I flicked my fingers twice more.

Lori turned her head and growled. "Are you helping him?"

"Just throw your sticks, dear lady."

Staring down her opponent, she threw the big stick into the middle. Now showboating, she waved the little stick in the air as the children in the crowd cheered. She threw it, and it landed behind the big stick so that, to win the contest, the top would need to travel around the big stick and settle closer to where I was sitting. A properly positioned left-handed release in my direction would set the top up to crawl around Lori's big stick. I signaled to Simok one more time. Though I think neither of us knew exactly what we were communicating to each other, he pivoted on his knees in the direction

I signaled. He wound the string around his homemade wooden top, looking to me for release approval. I nodded. The crowd oohed and aahed as the top landed on its mark and spun for a ten count. The top started wobbling and the children screamed in anticipation. The top made its final elliptical journey around the big stick and fell, nearly touching the little stick. It was victory for the home team! Simok jumped into the arms of his peers as the crowd cheered, except for the young lady in my lap. My knees ached, so I stood and reached out to Simok for a high five. My little charge, yawning, tugged at my pant legs and held out her arms. I picked her up.

Lori and Noy walked over to thank Simok for the game. I was left with a little girl in my arms, not sure who she belonged to or where the night was going. Finally, Colonel Kham appeared and translated my appreciation to the locals who had gathered around me, offering the sabaidee gesture of welcome on my behalf.

"They are thanking you for bringing your business to the town," he explained.

"Can you remind me what my business is?"

"You are the leader of the elite wildlife research team—the esteemed biologist Dr. Peter." He smiled and added, "Except to this little girl. To her, you are an uncle."

Noy returned to our conversation circle and spoke in Lao to Kham and then to me. "This little angel is Keiki. She followed us from the moment we arrived in the village. I learned from the older children where she lives. We should return her to her grandmother. It's getting late."

"I cannot go with you," Kham said. "There is still some distrust from the villagers, and it is aimed in my direction. They know that I am from the government. The Lao Air Force helicopters are returning tomorrow and will be followed by a convoy of soldiers to support our ground operations. I must prepare the elders for what is next. I hope that I will not have to make promises I cannot keep."

Lori popped in at that point. "I'll take her home. I know the house."

But Keiki held strong to my neck, so I said, "Feels like I have no choice but to go with you." I turned to Noy. "While I make this delivery, can you take care of my liberty buddy over there? Oh, and give this to him." I pulled a ten thousand kip note from my pocket with my free hand. "Chief Moore will know what it's for."

Noy turned to see the chief at a table, sitting with a group of adolescents challenging him to an arm-wrestling contest. "How cute!" she said as she plucked the note from my hand. "I will deliver this with pleasure."

As she walked away, Kham, Lori and I raised our eyebrows at each other. We all recognized the sparkle in Noy's eyes, and we smiled at each other, taking collective credit for an accidental matchmaking.

"Youth," Kham sighed. He then returned to our main purpose. "We should return to camp soon. I will finish with the elders in about an hour. Will you have returned the girl to her home by then?"

"Yes," I said, receiving a nod from Lori. The colonel wandered off, and Lori and I shuffled with Keiki on our way through the crowd and out the door.

We walked down the center of the main residential street, its contours illuminated from lighting reflecting off the low fog. Keiki was comforting to hold. I stroked her hair like I did Katya's. "Looks like she melted into your heart, sailor man," said Lori.

"She blew my cover. You heard Kham. I'm supposed to be Dr. Peter, esteemed wildlife biologist."

"Don't be fooled by Kham. He says that he is trying not to scare the villagers, but he's doing the opposite by lying. It's government patronization, and it's so disrespectful. Everybody knows who you are and why you are here. These are not simple people. They are disenfranchised. Noy knows this village better than the colonel. She talked to the women at the community center. She has their trust."

"Then why are we dancing around our purpose here? What human dynamic am I missing?"

As we walked, Lori explained. "There is a displaced population in this region—particularly in this village. They are Hmong, an ethnic minority that settled in the country's north after the Laotian civil war. Smaller enclaves are scattered here in the south of Laos and across the border in Vietnam. These Hmong were trapped between competing powers in the Vietnam War. They were not loyal to the Lao Kingdom at the time. Neither were they enamored by the promise of communism from North Vietnam. And they certainly were not welcomed by the other tribal factions that pepper the Mekong River basin. Many of these families have relatives that helped the CIA disrupt operations along the Ho Chi Minh Trail. At the war's end, they were abandoned by the US and persecuted by the Pathet Lao government that took over the country. Their plight resonates with me."

"How so?"

"On my tour in Afghanistan, I depended on a local woman—Duniya—to interpret for me. Years later, after a Taliban resurgence, I tried to get Duniya a special immigrant visa to get her out before the

Taliban caught up with her. The process for approval at the time was over two hundred days, and the line was hundreds deep. The NATO mission is fourteen years old now. Thousands of Afghanis risk their lives to help coalition forces. Engagement teams depend on them. I depended on them. But whenever a military mission goes south, our country turns blind and creates a bureaucracy that slows the process of extricating the helpers. These are real people who sign on to the US presence because mission success will make their lives better than any alternative. People are smart. Governments are not. Duniya didn't make it to the two-hundredth day." She sniffed and wiped a tear.

"I'm sorry for Duniya. And I'm sorry you didn't tell me about her before."

"There's a lot I don't tell you. Lots I don't tell anyone." She took a deep breath through her nose and exhaled into the night air. "I should unpack more of the load I carry."

"You can always talk to me," I said.

"I imagine your rucksack is pretty heavy, too. You don't need me adding to your weight."

Lori slowed our pace as she returned her focus to the here and now. "I sympathize with the locals here. War has scarred a generation, and the communists have largely ignored the needs of the people outside the big cities. The villagers here take care of each other. Colonel Kham may be a nice guy, but he's still an officer in a post-war communist regime. They don't trust Kham. They can't afford to. He's from the privileged class. Half of the villagers think he is out to frame them for insubordination and subversion."

"What about the other half?"

"They have things they want from the government. Access to

land. Freedom to clear cut forests and sell the wood. Exemption from wildlife protection rules for hunting. Electricity, water, internet, smartphones. Everything a developing world wants but can't have because the developed world makes the rules."

"It's the golden rule, Lori. If you own the gold, you get to rule." I was parroting a common saying used in the halls of the Pentagon. "What about Keiki here? Is she Hmong?"

"I believe so. Very subtle facial features give it away. I saw them immediately when she came to Noy and me."

We stopped in the middle of the road. "Do you know what you are looking for?" I said.

"I do. Noy got a clue from one of the children." Lori spun in a circle, inspecting the entries to all the homes on both sides of the street. She stopped the spin and pointed. "There. I see the house. You can tell by the porch."

The homes looked identical to me. "How do you know?"

"Check out the planter in the front. It's made from a bomb casing."

Sure enough, it was. The home's front porch was adorned with two flower planters made from the outer casings of American-manufactured cluster bombs.

Lori grabbed my arm to stop me from walking forward. Keiki stirred. "Can you promise to keep what we do tonight a secret?"

It was a ridiculous question. I held one of the highest security clearances in the US government. But a secret with Lori would be at an even higher level—and more personal. "I tied a bow for you with yellow caution tape around a black oak tree in the Woodland Hill woods. I promised that day I would find Michael and bring him home. And here we are, eleven years and millions of taxpayer dollars later, standing on a residential street of a mountain village in Laos. I keep my promises. And I know I can keep a secret. Just make it reasonable, please. I stink at lying."

"I need you to cover for me in the presence of Colonel Kham. And before we go into Keiki's house, I need you to promise to back me up on whatever I decide to do."

"Those are two very open-ended requests. Can you be more specific?"

"No. I just need to know that I have your support."

Without hesitation, I said, "You do. And that's no secret."

"Thank you." She breathed a sigh of relief. Stroking Keiki's hair, she whispered, "So sweet. She's a little angel. I remember you holding Charlie like that."

"You will explain all this spy craft to me later, won't you?"

"If I am right, I won't need to." She returned her gaze to the homes on the right side of the street. "I will say that I don't think Keiki just randomly gravitated to Noy and me. I believe she was sent."

"By whom?"

"Her grandmother."

I stroked Keiki's hair as she stirred in my arms. "Shhh. It's going to be all right. Uncle Peter's here."

Lori led us up the small stoop on the porch and whispered, "Sabaidee?"

A diminutive shadow emerged at the front entrance, backlit by candlelight from within the home. "Yes, yes," was the soft response from the occupant, confirming for me that we were expected.

Lori pulled me forward so Keiki was in view. The woman who

stepped out was more youthful than I had anticipated. Genuinely touched that I was holding Keiki, she guided me to a blanketed mat that I supposed was Keiki's bed. I laid the child down and turned to see Lori holding her shoes, staring at me like my mother used to when I did something wrong. It's a Lao custom to remove footwear before entering a home.

I offered a short nop bow to Keiki's grandma and removed my shoes. I took Lori's and my trekking boots out to the porch, where some long bamboo poles, ten feet or more in length, were stacked. I returned and the ladies were gesturing, holding a conversation with their hands to overcome the language barrier. I surmised that Lori had been asked about our relationship, and I was amused to watch her try to explain — without words — whether we were married, professional colleagues, friends, relatives, or something else. Noticing my return, the ladies giggled. I wish I knew what they had resolved.

Grandma directed us to sit on cushions in the room's center, while she wandered toward an alcove decorated with some flatware and pans. Lori whispered, "We should drink whatever is offered." I nodded in agreement. "And we must eat whatever is presented."

"Do I have to like it?" I asked with a smile.

Keiki's grandma returned with hot tea and a bowl of what looked like dates or even olives in the dim light. Lori lifted her glass to toast our host. In the spirit of diplomacy, we sipped. The tea was lukewarm and weak, so I focused on the hors d'oeuvres. Our host motioned me to eat first, so I speared the biggest prize in the bowl with a toothpick — a bug carcass smeared in oil. A cicada to be exact. An adult. Next to it were pupae and larvae also. The life cycle of the cicada was about to end as my evening meal. I paused to analyze my appetizer. Lori reached into the bowl, speared another cicada, and put it into her mouth. Not to be out done, I ate my morsel and chased it with a nymph. The taste was not awful. I had eaten—and subsequently hurled—much worse. To suppress any regurgitation reflex, I focused on the experience. I swallowed the bugs and sipped some more tea. Our host smiled at first, but soon her gaze became more studious. She stood up and disappeared into an unlit portion of the home. Lori grabbed my hand and said, "Wasn't that awesome? I always wanted to do that with you. Eat a cicada, I mean."

"That was high on my bucket list, too," I quipped, following up with a more serious question. "If that is Keiki's grandmother, where's her mom?"

"She could be in Sekong, working a clerical job and sending remittances to the village. Or she might be a victim of trafficking, maybe working a brothel in Thailand."

That second possibility was a mood killer. Our host returned with a folded piece of paper that she handed to Lori, who looked at it and handed it back. The two women traded nods and hand signals, once again penetrating the language barrier, leaving me in the dark. I kept my eyes forward but asked in a whisper to Lori, "What was on that paper?"

"It was your military biography printed from the Internet. She knows who you are."

"Does that matter?" I asked.

"I don't know," Lori responded while matter-of-factly reaching for another cicada and chomping it down. "Do me a favor," she said.

"What?"

"Leave."

"Now?"

"Yes. I'll stay in the village tonight. I feel a negotiation coming."

Bizarre as it sounded, I agreed. Getting information outside the bounds of our agreement with the Lao government meant that I should not be involved. I would have to keep this negotiation a secret from Colonel Kham—it could get all of us thrown out of the country.

I pointed to my watch and gestured my appreciation to our host for the hospitality. The cultural exchange was uplifting, but I had to remind myself that we had been lured to this home for a purpose. Both women escorted me out to the porch, where I sat next to the long poles and put my boots back on. Near the tip of one of the poles were a couple of cicada carcasses, held by tree sap. When I stood, Lori gave me a goodbye hug, whispering in my ear, "Don't wait up for me, and remember our agreement." She returned to the woman, took her hand, and disappeared into the home like they were sisters who hadn't seen each other in years.

Alone now in the middle of the dirt road, I donned the technology glasses, switched to night vision and looked back toward the town center. In the distance was the spectral glint of Chief Moore's glasses. Standing next to him were the silhouettes of Noy and Kham. As I approached their positions, I heard motorbikes revving. Soon three scooters arrived, one driven by the camp security guard, the others driven by locals who dismounted.

"Admiral, I have secured motorbikes to shorten our return to camp. Where is the distinguished lady?"

"She has been invited to stay in the village tonight. She thought it would be in our best interest, as a matter of diplomacy, not to turn down the hospitality."

Kham paused, then nodded. "I am not worried for her security, but we should stay together while here in the mountain region."

"I trust she will join us tomorrow," I said to placate him.

Pointing to his radio, Kham said, "Your brother called. He was very excited about the data collected on tonight's mission. The helicopters will arrive early in the morning for the next phase, but based on your brother's excitement, I called in the support convoy from the Sekong barracks. They are making haste in our direction. We will need their assistance if we are to penetrate the jungle for a recovery. They will also bring more ordnance disposal experts. The forest may be littered with cluster bombs and bomblets from the dark days of the past."

"Good call, Colonel. And should we find the missing US personnel, I have forces standing by in Hawai'i to complement your team. Let's get back to camp to see the data."

While Kham and I talked, Chief Moore, an experienced Harley aficionado, claimed the fanciest motor bike. Noy eagerly signed on as his riding partner.

Kham offered me a solo ride, which I accepted, leaving him to pair up with the guard. I loaned the guard my technology glasses as a goodwill gesture. Kham translated my words. "These will help you see better in the night."

The guard hesitated. I pressed the battery button, and he put them on after a brief inspection. I don't know what he said in Lao, but I know its four-letter equivalent in English. He really liked the glasses.

"I'll follow your lights, Colonel. Don't go too fast."

We mounted up, revved our vehicles, and motored toward

the hills, leaving the unanswered questions from the quaint, impoverished village for another day. After negotiating the switchback—not easy on a foggy night—I paused my bike for a moment to look back down the hill. My thoughts turned to Lori. Had I made the right decision in leaving her? The village lights had disappeared in the fog, as well as the other two bikes. I was alone on the fog-covered mountainside. I turned the bike motor off. I heard wind. I heard water trickling. I heard insects, lots of them. I had just eaten an insect with Lori. Lori's embrace of the whole situation made me shake my head and smile. I stopped worrying about her and just stood there, listening, absorbing, processing. Some rustling nearby shook me out of my thoughts. It was time to fire up the scooter and motor on, just in case any tigers were making a comeback from extinction.

I throttled the engine, puttering along. The fog was dense, and the scooter light was no help—it merely reflected off the moisture and created a sense of entrapment. I knew that if I was going uphill, I was likely headed in the right direction. But the road leveled, and I veered into the brush. I was experiencing vertigo, reminiscent of so many nights flying on instruments in the pre-technology days of my career.

"Hold on and don't let go," I mumbled to myself. Soon enough, I heard the putt-putt of a rescue scooter. It was Chief Moore, now alone, circling back to get me.

"The scooter stalled," I said.

"No worries, Admiral," said Moore. "The camp is three minutes away. Here's the other set of glasses."I put on the glasses and the fog disappeared.

"Thanks for coming back, Chief," I said.

"My honor, sir. I leave no shipmate behind."

STARING INTO THE ONCE BRILLIANT, now neglected campfire, I watched as embers crackled and twinkled for survival against the moisture of dense fog. I lacked any ambition to feed the fire as I sat across from Jason, who was wrapped in the thin sheath of a mylar thermal blanket. He was huddled over his laptop, scouring the data piped down from Clara that would determine the waypoints for tomorrow's low-altitude aerial survey. If we found wreckage, a member of the survey team would hoist down to mark the location and clear the area for ground retrieval teams from the inbound convoy. Chiefs Moore and Favors were my assets in this bilateral relationship. Colonel Kham would command everyone else as the host-nation officer-in-charge.

The next day would either validate the millions of taxpayer dollars I had committed to the project or bring me abject failure, along with a likely congressional inquiry into fraud and nepotism. Hero or villain. There was no in-between. Best efforts didn't matter now. I no longer owned the moment or had a say in the next decision.

I sat, feeling lost. Lori was off chasing a mysterious lead that either was or was not connected to our search. Kham had evaporated into the compound communication center to coordinate the convoy's mobilization. And Jason was living his dream, immersed in the technology that he had designed and developed. He was determined that Clara was up to this task. But I wallowed in self-doubt. A fog had descended over me.

Here in Laos, far from home, Lori had become Leslie. Keiki had become Katya. Charlie had drifted to Stacey and away from me. I was exactly where I wanted to be, yet I was nowhere in the same moment. I needed clarity. Jason must have intuited my internal cry for help over the crackling of the embers.

"I'm sending an email to Mom. What should I tell her?"

"You are supposed to be churning waypoints. The Royal Laotian Army and Air Force are arriving tomorrow, and they need a place to go and something to do."

"I'll get there. I'm waiting for a satellite with more bandwidth to pass overhead. I'll piggyback the email on the uplink."

"Whose satellite?"

"Company intellectual property. It's a little tiny CubeSat that we sent up about a month ago. You may have read about it in the classified portion of the brief."

"Sorry, it slipped by me. Does the satellite have a name?"

"Sure does." He looked up at me, his face blue as a ghost from the laptop reflection. "Stella."

"Cute," I said.

"Chez picked it out. It's her satellite anyway. Or her dad's. He owns the company, but it will be hers whenever he checks out."

"Good for Chez. And funny at the same time. I wouldn't have put her down as the CEO of a Japanese tech company."

"How so?"

"Well, two days ago she was dragging your bags, checking on Mabel, obsessing over Clara. Two months from now — or 'whenever her father checks out' — you'll be the one toting her bags."

"I will, big brother. And I won't mind toting them at all." He closed the computer. "The way it is now is the way she wants it. She's smart.

She wants to be undercover, a clandestine CEO-in-training. She flies me all around the world and learns about innovation and opportunity from observing people. She believes that having fewer, more intimate relationships is better than having a broad-based, loose-knit network. Bonds are stronger if the team is smaller. And I agree."

"Did Dad teach you that?"

"Him—and you. You keep your friends close. And they value that closeness."

I didn't thank him for the compliment, but he knew I appreciated it. I moved the conversation sideways. "Are you and Chez…intimate? Anything I need to tell Mom?"

"All business for now. If anything changes, Mom will be the first to know. You'll be second." He opened his laptop and started typing. "Stella's in range. Uplink enabled. Another five minutes and we'll have your lat-longs for tomorrow."

"Where's Clara?" I asked.

Jason kept his head down but pointed straight up to the sky. "Right above us at about one hundred feet."

I looked up as he tapped a few buttons on the keyboard to engage Clara's spotlight, which punched through the fog. "Cool," I muttered. "And she talks to satellites, too?"

"She's just a relay. Stella is talking to Mabel on the tarmac in Vientiane. Mabel is digesting data and sending us what we need through Clara. Clara gets me what I need here on the laptop. And I give it to you. Every device has a piece of the knowledge chain, but no one device knows everything. That way, if bits of communication are intercepted, the pieces independently look like gibberish."

"My brother is Batman."

"I prefer Ironman, but without the burden of global security. That's your job."

I curled up in my blanket as the fire reduced to embers. "Yes, it is. For now."

"So, what should I tell her?"

"Who?

"Mom. The email. Hurry before the CubeSat moves on."

"Let her know we are fine. The mission is going well." Jason typed as I spoke. "Send her our love. From everyone out here. And from Charlie, too. Don't forget Charlie. And Katya."

Jason finished typing with a flurry and hit the return button. "Shit," I said. "Did you get Leslie in there?"

"I did."

"Thanks, Jason."

"It's Ironman, if you don't mind."

I decided to resurrect the fire, so I stood to get a piece of wood. I lost my footing in the fog and tripped on my first step. "Let me help," Jason said. With a few taps on the laptop, Clara appeared ten feet over my head, shining a light that allowed me to move about as if in daylight. She followed me to the wood pile, where I spied an embarrassed Chief Moore and Noy in an embrace.

Back at the fire, I laid the log on top and prepped the kindling. I grinned at Jason. "Can Clara start a fire for us?"

"I haven't installed the flamethrower yet, so use this." He tossed a fire-starter match kit my way.

"This is so old school," I said. "The Pentagon won't buy your toy until you put a flamethrower on it."

Clara's light show drew the attention of the US team, who

wandered from the dark corners of the campground to the now brisk and brilliant fire. Chez took control of Clara from Jason's laptop through a remote device that switched the drone's command to the virtual-reality goggles.

"All right, bomb guy," said Chez to Chief Favors. "Let's see you land her."

"With pleasure. I was getting tired of spying on Chief Moore."

Noy sat close to Moore, smiling and hanging on his arm.

"Just land the damn thing without crashing," Moore said. He put his arm around Noy and made no secret of their new connection.

Jason called the impromptu meeting to order. "Speaking of crashes, Admiral, I believe we have strong evidence of at least five crash sites. Two of them have stunted forest growth that might be attributable to intense magnesium fire. That was a factor you asked us to consider in the data crunch."

"What's the significance of magnesium?" Noy asked.

"Magnesium alloys are used in many helicopter engine and transmission components," said Chez. "The alloys are just as strong as their aluminum or titanium counterparts but are extremely lightweight and, therefore, cost effective."

Chief Moore chimed in. "Magnesium fires burn hotter and last longer than those fueled by trees because you can't put them out with water. A magnesium fire is so intense, it could delay a forest's regrowth by years. Am I correct?" He looked to Chez and she nodded in affirmation.

Favors filled in the technical details. "Magnesium fires actually cause hydrogen and oxygen molecules to separate. The magnesium bonds with the oxygen to form magnesium oxide, which keeps burning. But the hydrogen gas is now on its own and exposed to the heat of the fire. Hydrogen burns quite easily. Adding water, like a torrential rainstorm, to a magnesium fire gives you a hydrogen explosion." He used both hands and a puff of air for visual effect. "It's like the Hindenburg airship."

It was Noy who said what I was thinking. "I'm sure glad Lori's not here for this conversation."

"And we must assume she won't be here for tomorrow's mission," I added without elaboration. "Thank you, chiefs, for the technical explanation. I would like us to consider a sudden-impact crash scenario as our primary hypothesis.

"Fog like this can be disorienting. An aircraft smashing into the terrain would immediately initiate the fire that Chief Favors described and alter the forest's growth profile."

Chief Moore raised a finger to get my attention. "There's another scenario that would result in a fire, Admiral. In our Special Operations training for personnel recovery missions, we always include the possibility that the aircraft took fire from an air-to-ground missile or a rocket-propelled grenade but was still flyable. If they went down on their own power, the crew may have set fire to the aircraft to make it look like a shoot-down. In that scenario, there were likely survivors, who were then forced to evade capture." The campfire crackled as Moore's words hung in the air.

I broke the long silence. "Even if they survived, our mission doesn't change. We find the aircraft and then we look for more clues." I needed the team to focus on our task, but I admit that thinking about an eight-man crew evading capture—and surviving for any length of time—was disheartening.

Jason handed me his laptop. "I tagged two points on the map, Alpha and Bravo. Point Alpha fits your hillside-crash scenario, Admiral. It's about three kilometers from here, over one ridge and straight east toward the Vietnamese border. It rests on very steep terrain. You'll need to hoist a crew down through the trees to get a visual sighting. Point Bravo is not far from here. It's quite accessible from the village by a long walk on a few dirt paths. It fits both profiles. There was an intense fire at Bravo, for sure."

"Then the decision is easy," I said. "We split the team and search both locations. Chief Moore?"

"Sir?"

"You and I will man the helicopters. If weather and terrain permit, we'll insert at Point Alpha and see what we can find."

"Chief Favors?"

"Sir?"

"You lead the ground team to Point Bravo. Noy will go with you and keep the tigers at bay."

"Yes, sir." Favors saluted with a smile.

"Chez?"

Chez smiled, raised her hand, and whispered politely, "Present."

"Can you support both missions from here? Solo? I have alternate tasking for Jason.

She nodded. "Solo is easy."

"Also, do we have enough generator juice to recharge Clara?"

Chez nodded again. "I made the request to Colonel Kham for several generators earlier. He assures me there will be more than enough for our purpose. I also secured a private agreement on behalf of my company to leave some of the generators and fuel stores behind for the village to use. I tacked on a few other sundry requests on behalf of the local population."

"That was very generous. I think the village will appreciate the gesture."

Jason eyed me. "What's my assignment for tomorrow, boss?"

"Find Lori first thing in the morning. Stay with her under all circumstances. It will be an especially tough day for her."

Per our bilateral mission arrangement, I needed Kham to sign off on the ground-infiltration plan. Later that evening, I briefed him in private. Each team would use a Chez-Tech electronic tablet to communicate. Clara, with Stella's help, would keep us updated on the mission operational picture and coordinate flight waypoints.

Kham was more than accommodating. "The mission is in your hands, Admiral. I have directed the crews to follow your orders. They will be here shortly after first light. In the meantime, I will be in the village, working with the elders to prepare for the convoy arrival."

He must have read the concern on my face as to who was footing the bill for the convoy. "And don't worry, Admiral, the forces arriving tomorrow serve at the pleasure of the Lao People's Democratic Republic."

I had a distinct feeling that the private negotiation Chez had had with Kham went way beyond generators, fuel, and sundries. I thanked him and added, "Your crews are very professional, and they have all my respect. I hope our two countries will bond over this common mission that reconciles the past."

14

Mission Day 6
Ta Vang, Laos

By sunrise, Noy and Chief Favors left camp with Kham to meet the advance team of Laotian soldiers assigned for the ground trek to Point Bravo. Chez and I reviewed the weather, mission details, and a few contingency plans in case there were any outlier challenges to our operations—the "known unknowns" in Pentagon-speak. In one such scenario, Clara—really Chez and all her technology—would take over the mission if something were to happen to me. My absence would precipitate a safe and orderly return to base for all units not engaged in an active rescue.

Pilot to pilot, neither Chez nor I mentioned the word crash, but that's what we were talking about. It was surreal to think about crashing while looking for a crash site.

I hitched a scooter ride down to the helicopter pad with Chief Moore. Villagers once again assembled in curiosity as the two Hueys from the day before landed. I huddled with the English-speaking crew of the lead chopper that would be my ride to Point Alpha.

I briefed both crews on the use of the electronic flight tablets. In addition to updating the operational picture in real time, Clara would track the Bravo team location, weather phenomena, and any low-slow air traffic entering our airspace. As a courtesy, I had unlocked the encryption of known smuggling routes to and from Vietnam, as well as unexploded ordnance locations. The latter bonded Chief Moore and his Lao Air Force counterpart; they would be the first to ride the hoist to the forest floor.

Jason — who had left before sunrise to track down Lori — jogged to the landing zone and motioned to me for a private conversation.

"Lori's nowhere to be found. Not at the house you described. Not in the community center. I found a boy who spoke some French. He took me around the village and through the residential section. There was barely a soul. The few people we found wouldn't fess up to her whereabouts. Something weird is going on."

"Any sign of the little girl at the house?"

"I asked the boy. He knows Keiki. Her *ma tao*, or grandmother, is named Alika. But no one was there. The house was empty."

"Any shoes on the porch?"

"I don't think so. Like I said, the neighborhood was empty."

"How about the poles? They had long bamboo poles on the porch that I think the women use to hunt cicadas."

"I don't recall seeing any poles, but I can check again."

"Don't bother. You would have noticed the poles."

Lori had left the village, I assumed by choice. "Jason, can Clara take on another search mission?"

"She's built for multitasking."

"See if Clara can find Lori. She's likely in the forest with a group. But don't post her position on the tablet. Just let me know when you find her. Tell me over the radio. Use a codeword, not her name. I'll explain later."

"What name? What codeword?"

"Naming things is your specialty."

Jason looked genuinely panicked. "Not people! I can't give nicknames to people."

"Why not?"

"It might hurt their feelings. I can't deal with that."

I put my hand on his shoulder. "Okay, calm down," I said. "She's not in trouble, and she is not in danger. We just want to find her. If I say the phrase 'spice rack,' you reply 'cinnamon.' And add 'sweet' or 'sour' depending on whether she is located."

"'Cinnamon' is Lori, right?"

"That's her new call sign. Now get going. Tell Chez what's going on." Just beyond the Huey's rotor arc was the motor scooter Chief Moore and I had ridden down the campsite hill. I directed Jason with my eyes. Smiling, he sprinted to it. "You go, Ironman," I yelled. "And don't name the bike."

"Too late," he shouted back. "It's Theodore!" With that, he revved up the motor and spun dirt.

As he and the bike zoomed past, Chief Moore shouted, "Hey, that's my ride!"

Within minutes, I was airborne, strapped into the crew station's right-side jump seat. I donned a loaner helmet that was plugged in so I could hear both the outside radio calls coming into the cockpit and the internal crew dialogue. Clara had established her position over Point Alpha and had optimized the location for hoist operations based on the sloping terrain, wind, and tree height. The pilot flew at near-constant altitude below occasional puffs of clouds, and above the undulating forested terrain.

The copilot stared back at me, pointing to the tablet. "Admiral, we are five minutes to Point Alpha. But the drone is heading in a different direction. Should we follow it?"

"No. It will return if we need it." I figured an explanation from Jason would come over the common radio frequency. My first hunch was that Jason was redirecting Clara to look for the heat signatures of cicada-hunting villagers. Lori would likely be with them. But the garbled radio call, scrambled by the mountainous terrain, came instead from Chief Favors. None of us could make out what he was saying, so our pilot radioed the wingman copter with orders to climb in altitude and relay the message.

In the meantime, we arrived at Point Alpha. The pilot banked the aircraft so I could have a good look. In the middle of the steep terrain was a scrape in the hillside. Had we found the impact sight? Chief Moore prepared for the hoist ride down. Together, he and his Lao counterpart discussed an acceptable drop point. They settled on one down the slope from the scrape, close to a spot with small trees. A third crewman hooked a metallic, jungle-penetrating device to the end of the hoist. As the Huey pulled into a hover, the pilot authorized commencement of hoisting operations.

Moore and the Lao crewman straddled the flip-down seats of the penetrator outside of the cabin door. They locked their safety carabiners to the hoist assembly and released their gunner belts for the cable ride down about one hundred feet. Once on the ground, the Lao crewman radioed the cockpit "ops normal," and the hoist was retrieved, leaving the two to carry on with their search. I watched out the cabin door and tried to visualize Michael and his crew crashing on this hillside. Chief Moore radioed that they were expanding their hunt up the hill. It would take some time for them to reach the objective site.

Blending in with the engine whine, thumping blades, and wind blast was a radio call in Lao from the wingman. The copilot translated. "Admiral, the ground team reported an explosion near Point Bravo. All movement has been halted."

"Lori," I said out loud, but not on the intercom. The pilot departed the hover and climbed to a holding altitude to conserve fuel and await my direction.

I asked the pilot over the intercom, "Can Dash-2 stay here and retrieve our ground team?"

"I'll make it so. Where do you need to be?"

"Fly to the drone," I said. I shuffled forward in the cabin and poked my head over the shoulder of the copilot. "I need to make a radio call."

At the direction of the copilot, the hoist operator switched my communication settings to the tactical broadcast frequency.

"Ironman, this is Passed Ball."

"Ironman here. Loud and clear," Jason responded.

"Update Bravo status."

"Bravo team reported multiple ordnance explosions in their vicinity. Source unknown. Team is unaffected but holding in place."

"I have two assets on the ground at Alpha. Dash-2 will pick them up. We're inbound to Point Bravo to investigate. Interrogative spice rack?"

"Cinnamon sour. Clara's working on it."

"Roger," I acknowledged and then asked the pilot-in-command on the intercom, "If my brother can locate the source of the explosion, can you fly me there?"

The pilot gave me a thumbs up. "I'd be glad to check it out."

"Thank you. Keep flying to the drone." I pointed to the moving dot on the tablet that represented Clara's position. The pilot nosed the aircraft down and added power to attain maximum airspeed.

The airwaves remained silent as the minutes creeped by. Before I could ask for an update, Jason called. "Cinnamon sweet. Clara's on station at three hundred feet. I'll light her up."

The pilot pointed forward. "Strobe light, twelve o'clock."

"That's Clara," I said to the pilot. I followed up with a radio call to Jason, "Tallyho, Clara."

Jason came back. "Once on top, you should see Cinnamon. The zone is too small to land. Can you hoist a crew down?"

"Affirmative," I answered. The pilot maneuvered the Huey below Clara's altitude and circled the drop zone. I pivoted to the cabin door and radioed Jason. "We're on top."

From an altitude of about one-hundred-and-fifty feet, we saw Lori waving a white dress affixed to the end of a long bamboo pole. I notified the pilot, "It has to be me. I need to go down the hoist."

The crewman hooked me to the jungle penetrator and helped me straddle one of three flaps on the device. He pointed to my survival radio and shouted, "Call me when you are on the ground. I'll come down if she needs medical attention." He pushed me out the door and into the rotor slipstream.

The windblast jolted my memories of past hoist rides. In training and during rescue, I always rode the cable up and out of water—not down to solid ground. I kept my eyes forward and focused, anticipating hitting the ground. This was no time to screw up. I crouched into my familiar catcher squat and timed my landing to the trees that were growing larger in my field of view. On ground impact, I rolled with the penetrator device and then detached it from my safety carabiner. I looked up to the hoist operator through thick dust and blowing grass. He pointed to his helmet, reminding me to call him.

I shouted into my radio, signaling him with a thumbs up, "I'm clear!" The penetrator rose off the ground, swinging madly in the downwash. I stayed crouched as the device returned to the helicopter and the crew maneuvered away. The downwash dissipated, leaving the flying grass and dust to settle in the natural wisps of wind.

I stood and looked for Lori, but she was not in sight. I took my helmet off and called for her. "Lori!" No response. "Lori! Where are you?" Still no response. I radioed Jason. "Ironman, this is Passed Ball. I need eyes on Cinnamon."

A shout came from the woods in front of me. It was Lori's voice. She stayed in the woods. "Call them off, Peter. Make the drone go away!"

"Lori? What's going on? Are you all right?"

"I'm fine. Everything is fine. Remember your promise, Peter."

"I remember." I did not advance. I sensed a hostage situation, and she—and maybe me—were in the middle of something outside the scope of our mission. I called Jason. "Jason, I need all forces to standoff from my location by at least two miles. Send Clara away."

"Copy that, boss."

I looked up to see Clara's strobe light extinguish as she headed away. "Lori, we are good now," I shouted to the woods. She emerged, walking first and then running. We embraced as we did at Woodland Hill—an embrace that threw all confusion and quandary aside. At this moment, I knew she was more than safe. "You found him, didn't you?"

She was too choked up to answer. I stroked back her hair and held her longer. As she cried into my flight suit, I glanced up to the wooded boundary from where Lori had emerged and spotted a little girl in a white dress. "Keiki?"

Lori, still in my arms, turned and waved to the little girl, who was soon joined by her grandmother, Alika. "Alika showed me where Michael is. His whole crew, too. But we must give her and Keiki time to return to the village. Kham can't know that they helped."

"How much time do they need?"

"Can we wait here for half an hour?"

"We own the information. We own the mission. We can wait as long as you want."

"Thirty minutes is good. Let's just sit here, and I'll tell you about my day."

Alika was not alone. She had helpers who remained in the shadows. The women had been aware of the Bravo team's advancement. When the team had gotten too close to a hidden encampment that included the remains of the Jolly Green flight crew, the village women improvised a scare-and-delay tactic that worked. Accessing a store of old cluster bomblets, they had triggered the ordnance explosion.

I radioed Jason and asked him to transmit orders to all airborne and ground units. I directed the Bravo team to return to the village to work with Kham and organize the convoy for recovery operations the next day while the Dash-2 crew recovered Chief Moore and his Lao counterpart. At Point Alpha, they had found the wreckage of a Laotian T-28D fixed-wing piston-engine aircraft but no evidence of a pilot or crew. The scars of civil and regional war fought decades prior still haunted the mountains and deep forest terrain around us. But one very deep scar — inflicted on the soul of a rambunctious, cinnamon-haired tomboy from a town eight thousand miles away from this place — had finally begun the slow process of healing.

We sat in the downwash-flattened grass. I had questions but waited for her to talk first.

"Alika's parents were part of a CIA sleeper cell that helped downed pilots. Michael's crew was shot down. Michael survived but was hurt badly. He was manning the door gun. A grenade launcher struck the tail rotor. He was thrown, hanging outside the aircraft as it spun out of control. He was pinned to the outside of the helicopter as they crashed through the trees."

"How do you know this?"

"Alika saw it. She was there. She is my age."

"How long was Michael alive?"

"Long enough to convince a little girl that he wouldn't harm her. Alika's parents managed to get the crew out, hide their bodies, and burn the aircraft before the Pathet Lao forces arrived. Alika thinks the crew perished in the crash or very shortly thereafter.

"She claimed Michael would not leave his crew. She was with Michael as he died. He and the crew are buried in an abandoned tunnel just through the woods. The tunnel is on a portion of the Ho Chi Minh Trail that was cut off from the network and repurposed for the Hmong sleeper cell."

"How did she know who you were?"

"Alika said Michael told her about me. He knew some basic Lao." Tears reappeared as she pulled a faded elementary school picture of herself from her pocket. "He carried this picture of me inside the liner of his flight suit. He gave it to her." She looked to the sky with a pensive smile. "Michael told Alika that one day his sister would come and get him. And that she would like to meet me."

Lori looked me in the eye. "And here I am."

I held her in the field until we heard a humming up above. I ventured a glance at the sky. "Clara's here. The team is worried about you, and we need to get Michael and his crew home."

"He's safe tonight. Alika has guaranteed that the bodies will be protected until tomorrow. We can head back to camp. I need to call Patty."

I radioed the flight crew, who came and lowered the jungle penetrator from the hoist along with headgear for Lori's safety. I showed Lori how to straddle the penetrator and secured her safety harness. She shouted over the helicopter noise, "Don't worry. I've done this more times than you know."

"Got it, but I'm still going to hold you on the way up." I signaled to the hoist operator to commence the lift. Our arms entwined as we rose above the trees to the rescue helicopter. Between the altitude of the helicopter and the rescue hoist's speed, we were at the crew door in about thirty seconds. I cherish those thirty seconds—and will for the rest of my life.

On the flight home from Laos, I finally found the words to conclude a poetic diatribe I had started fourteen years prior.

The Answer

I face the mirror and cannot hide
internal anguish masked by pride;
It is time for me to share
a burden with those who care
to join my search to find the answer.
If I write the world a short letter,
    Pithy and sharp, nothing better;
        Telling of perils I did survive
To reclaim hope, my spirit revived
          I am ready now to find the answer.
If I write the world a good book
    That invites a respectful look;
        The authored words that I do yield
        Can be a useful sword and shield
          That can help us find the answer.
If I write the world a stoic song,
    not a lecture of what is wrong;
but a map to aid our flight
that can lead us to the light,
and maybe there we'll find the answer.
For when we've reached the trail's end
for a cause we swore to defend,
all effort must be prolonged,
and forever must live the song
and the search to find the answer.

CYCLE FOUR

Intrepidity

Intrepidity is a quality of spirit that enables one to face danger or pain without showing it.

15

2021
Arlington National Cemetery, Virginia
Memorial Day

Every blade of grass was lush from the earlier rainfall. The trees, dark as deciduous green can get, spread from mighty trunks. Cotton ball clouds gathered on the horizon, but the sky became infinitely blue as my gaze strayed upward. If it were any other day, it would've been perfect. Brood X added intrigue to the perfection, providing a synchronized wall of sound like an audio version of the wave performed by baseball fans in a stadium. If baseball were our purpose, the game would start early and might never stop. This Memorial Day, however, I reflected upon games not played.

I had managed to get Michael's grave placed in Section 64 of Arlington National Cemetery, within line of sight of the Pentagon Group Burial Marker. A text from Leslie notified me to be on the lookout for a spunky eleven-year-old headed my way. I spied Katya through my prescription aviator glasses, prancing over the uneven grass surface that bore the weight of thousands of simple white marble headstones.

Once on the unpaved maintenance path, she picked up to a trot and then ran full sprint and jumped into my arms, joining me at Michael's gravesite.

"Oh, my little Katybug!" I said, and twirled her back to the ground. When I had last checked on Leslie, she had been staring into the granular depths of her late husband's name inscribed on the group marker for September 11, 2001.

"Has Momma finished her visit?"

Katya squinted at me. "She's sad. I think she needs more alone time with Uncle Mark."

"You are so smart, Katya. We'll wait a little longer for her. Thank you for coming with us to say goodbye to Uncle Mark and Uncle Michael."

"Momma says you gave Uncle Mark the nickname 'Trashman.'"

I smiled. "It was a name given out of love. He was my best friend." It was too complicated to discuss how naval aviators get their nicknames. Too embarrassing also. Mark had taken the fall for a sailor who mistakenly threw a piece of classified material into the outgoing trash. The paper caught a gust of wind and flew from the parking lot dumpster to the commanding officer's parking space. Razz had squeezed every ounce of humor out of that episode while maintaining the appropriate level of seriousness about security violations.

"And Momma says he called you 'Passed Ball.' Do you like that name?"

"To be honest, honey, no. It reminds me of a mistake I made playing baseball in college. I dropped a pitch in an important game, and the winning run scored."

Again, it was too complicated to tell her it was during a College World Series playoff game, when infamy and a professional career were on the line. Baseball is a game of errors and missed opportunities. A big-league career hinges on a player being perfect when perfection is required. I called the pitch—a simple curve ball on a two-strike count. The third-base runner was no threat to steal and one last strike would get us out of the inning. I was due up in the top of the tenth and was thinking ahead to being the hero at bat—not the goat with the glove.

The curve ball caught the batter off guard. He swung as the pitch dropped a foot in front of the plate. I went down on my knees to block the pitch as I had done a thousand times before and the baseball skipped through my legs. The runner advanced to first base on my dropped strike—and the runner on third scored. Game over. Season over. No future career in baseball.

"Were your teammates mad at you?"

"Yeah, but I think they forgave me," I told her, though I have doubts to this day and try hard to suppress the memory.

"Sometimes I make mistakes and feel bad," she said.

My daughter's honesty caught my attention. I took off my glasses and squatted down to her level. "Is there something that is bothering you right now? Do you want to tell me about it?"

She twirled her hair. "I'm scared about moving to California. Sometimes I think nobody will like me because they won't know me. What do I do if they don't like me?"

"Well, *I* think you are the greatest person on this planet. I know it's hard to move to a new neighborhood and go to a new school. I did it once too. But I learned a few tricks on how to meet new friends. You can use my tricks, and maybe a friend you meet will become your best friend forever." I made a mental note to pack her softball glove in our travel bag so it would always be available for catch on our drive across the nation.

"Honeybun, I can't make those uneasy feelings disappear, but I promise I will try to help if you promise me that you will tell me when you have those feelings. Promise?"

She smiled. "Promise." We proceeded with our secret promise handshake—a complicated set of high and low fives, forward and backhand slaps, synchronized finger-pointing, a minor hip dip, and one awkward (for me) twirl. I squeezed her tight and rocked her until she giggled. "Come on, Katya, let's walk to Momma and get ready for this afternoon."

"Can I say goodbye to Uncle Michael first?"

"Of course." I stepped away from the headstone to give her alone time. Though she had never met Michael, he had become a part of her life. His story—reinforced by a close relationship with Charlie and Lori—was part of our family's narrative too.

"Daddy, look what flew on top of Michael."

I glanced back and atop Michael's headstone was a single Brood X cicada. As Katya picked it up and held it in her hand, I reflected on the man she calls "Uncle Michael" and how we finally found him.

Leslie's arrival snapped me out of my thoughts. Her eyes were red, her cheeks dry. "We can leave now," she said. "I'm done crying. Let's get going and get this day over with."

I hugged her as Katya set her cicada free to join the airborne fleet peppering the sky. We joined hands as a family and started our walk to the Army base parking lot at the west end of the cemetery. "Daddy, can I ride with you in the camper?" asked Katya.

"Not yet, honeybun," I said. "I want to test it one more time before we leave for California." The camper was our family's new, all-electric Winnebago van, decked out with driver-less technology courtesy of Jason and a Little Creek-based start-up. Once again, I was going to be a test pilot—this time for Jason as part of a Department of Defense innovation competition.

Starting the next day, Leslie and I would be monitoring the RV as it drove itself on a meandering path to national parks and remote military bases across this great nation. The actual competition part wouldn't start until midnight, when teams of hackers from their college dorm rooms or parents' basements would try to infiltrate Jason's spoof-proof technology and ruin our hard-earned, post-pandemic vacation. I have never been steered wrong by my brother. On this trip, I trusted him to keep me on track once again, this time with my family aboard.

On our walk to the parking lot, I reminded Katya of the task that had to be accomplished before midnight—an important task Jason had entrusted only to her. "Have you come up with a name for the camper?" I asked.

"I have. But I want to tell Charlie first." That said, she ran ahead to our car, which was parked next to the camper, giving Leslie and me a moment of privacy.

I turned to my wife. "Would you mind finding a diversion for Katya and arriving at Woodland Hill a bit after me? Maybe half an hour? I need some time alone with Charlie."

"Sure," she said. "I can do that. We can take one last trip to the old neighborhood and say goodbye to our house. I'll stop by the sandwich shop and grab some food for the drive." She turned to face me and held both my hands, looking down at the ground at first. "If it's all right with you, I'll stay in the camper during the ceremony. I know the Myers event is very important to you and to Charlie's family." She raised her eyes to meet mine. "I'm just not sure I can handle more sadness today. I said goodbye to Mark, and I don't want to look backward anymore. I want to start our new journey and head west as soon as possible."

"I agree," I replied. "The ceremony will help with my goodbyes. And Charlie *is* my son. I want to make sure his head is on straight before he deploys." We embraced. As I stroked her hair, the tender moment was interrupted by a cicada I found entangled in her locks.

Leslie drove off with Katya toward the main gate of the base while I programmed the RV with destination coordinates for Woodland Hill and Myers Charter Elementary School. I had complete confidence in Jason's technology, and the RV itself was an authorized driver-less vehicle licensed to operate in every state along our route to San Francisco, where we would put down new roots. Still, a retired admiral caught on base-security footage with no hands on the steering wheel—as if in the act of texting—would not look good.

I gave into my anxiety and placed my hands on the wheel for appearance's sake as the Winnebago drove itself through the gate and onto the state road. But from that moment on, I was hands off, full trust. Like a Sea King helicopter on autopilot, the RV hummed along on its own, merging into traffic and finding its groove on the interstate in the crowded westbound center lane.

I settled into the real purpose of why I wanted to be alone. I pulled out the plastic award container that protected the Silver Star medal for Michael that I would present to Patch later that day. I detached the ribbon and medal assembly from its casing and dangled it near the windshield for all traffic to see. Its brilliant red, white, and blue fabric attached to a shiny five-point emblem of valor reminded me of my mentor, Razz, and his combat-rescue mission to recover a jet pilot in North Vietnam.

The author of Razz's rescue-award citation told a much different story from what Commander Rasmussen had shared with his junior officers. The award's narrative was smooth, describing Razz's coolness and calm while under attack. It stated as a matter of fact: "In the face of intense enemy fire, Lieutenant Rasmussen commenced a low-level flight and turned on his landing lights to facilitate the search for a downed pilot. Although his aircraft was repeatedly targeted, he continued the search until the pilot was located."

If I had no knowledge of the H-3 helicopter he'd been flying, I might have guessed from the text's description that he was alone in a fortified air vehicle, immune to bullets and grenade launchers.

But I knew the real story. His tale — told to a packed ready room of combat-thirsty, naive junior pilots — was fraught with confusion, chaos, and disorientation. From Razz's recounting, the downed pilot had vectored him and his Sea King crew to the wrong landing zone. The pilot heard the engines and rotor noise but could not spot the helicopter in the night unless the crew turned on some lights. When they did, enemy gun fire rained from every direction. Razz flew under the heavy fire to three landing zones before the downed pilot could hop aboard.

At the end of his story, Razz emotionally complimented his crew for their stick-to-itiveness, complaining that the crew — all junior to him—received the prestigious Bronze Star for combat action, a "lesser" award than his.

The same four words start every Silver Star citation: *"For conspicuous gallantry and intrepidity."* All senior military leaders are conversant in award-writing, and as a fan of poetry and song, I love words. When I drafted Michael's award citation, it was not hard to chisel a story that met the criteria for conspicuous gallantry—he was the knight who rescues, as Alika later testified.

But intrepidity is a word that required a deeper dive into Michael's actions. Intrepidity is a quality of spirit that enables one to face danger or pain without showing it. Michael demonstrated that quality long before he even set foot on that Jolly Green helicopter in 1972—enlisting in the Army in 1970 during wartime. Volunteering for covert operations in Laos with a unit whose mission was to rescue fellow soldiers and airmen from danger and pain. Refusing to leave his downed flight crew near Ta Vang—and securing an ally in Alika, who would guarantee their dignified return home, all while mortally wounded himself. His conduct was truly worthy of the word. I'm glad the Secretary of the Army agreed, and I am indebted to Razz for pulling the strings necessary to get her signature on the award.

A subtle beep from the RV's remote-piloting system alerted me to the approaching exit for Woodland Hill. There were still a few miles of back roads to drive, so I returned the award to my backpack and took a deep breath. It was time to demonstrate my complete confidence in Jason and his technological wizardry. I unbuckled my seatbelt and left the driver's seat to change into my service uniform summer whites. I wanted to dignify the ceremony, but I also wanted to look spiffy for the web stream of my very first podcast.

16

Woodland Hill, Virginia

"Admiral, what are you staring at?" Charlie said, as he double-timed up the ridge and popped to attention in front of me, delivering a crisp salute.

I returned the gesture and took off my combo cover hat, motioning him to remove his garrison cap.

"I'm looking at Clarence." I pointed to Jason's drone holding its position about thirty feet above us. "We're going to live stream today's ceremony on YouTube for the teachers and the kids. I want to get the words right for my first podcast."

"Cool. Is Uncle Jason online?"

"Not yet. He and Nana will join us in thirty minutes." I pressed icons on my watch to put the drone in a hover with the camera off. "Thanks for coming early. Check out this bench."

"A four-seater. Looks great."

"It sends the message that there is always room for the missing man."

Charlie smiled. "Papi is going to love it. I can't wait till he gets here. It will be the first time he's seen me in uniform."

I smiled too. "It looks good on you, son. Though navy blue would have looked better."

He laughed, withholding comments about our inter-service rivalry.

"Your mother said you have a set of orders to Pendleton. Sounds like you're headed to the 1st Marine Division, Papi's old unit. When do you ship out?"

"Thursday. Zero six hundred."

"You ready?"

"Oorah!"

"Seriously, Charlie," I said. "Are you ready?"

"What do you mean, Pops?"

"Was my advice worthwhile? Did I give you good gouge?"

"It worked in boot camp," he said. "No reason to believe I'm not prepared for my next assignment."

"Love the double negative, son. The gouge might appear good but remember the corollary."

"I know, I know. 'Live by the gouge, die by the gouge.' Heard that all the time from the drill instructors."

"Gunny sergeants. God bless them." My brain flashed back forty years to when I was a confused, razor-thin college graduate who volunteered to be parachuted into the dense summer humidity of Pensacola, Florida. Aviation Officer Candidate School was fourteen weeks of hell led by screaming gunnery sergeants adhering to a mindless boot camp script that was meant to break you down as a human being and build you back up as a naval officer. Charlie brought me back to the present. "Am I missing anything, Pops?"

"Tools? Training? Technology?"

"Got them."

"Risk? Rights? Respect?"

"Got them."

"Budgeting and benefits?" He nodded.

"Teamwork? Time management?"

"Those, too."

"Physically fit?" He flexed his biceps.

"Stable genius?"

"Head screwed on straight."

"Spiritually grounded?"

"Hell, yeah!"

"Confident?"

"Getting there."

"Motivated?"

"Always."

"Then my job is done."

Charlie stood and primped his uniform, trying to hide his wry smile, and looked up at the drone. "I have some time before Thursday to hang out with Mom. She probably has a war story or two I could use on deployment. We might even read some of your poems. Thanks for sending the link. I get a kick out of bad poetry."

"I've written lots of poems, Charlie. They can't all be bad."

"You're right. Not all bad. Just most of them."

I laughed. "I use a swarming tactic with my writing, Charlie. If I launch a thousand words at a reader, a few are bound to hit the mark and make an impression."

"I bet they will, Pops. Keep at it."

He pivoted the discussion. "I have a special request for your next podcast episode. Can you throw me a story or two about you and Mom? I want to know more about you guys. At Michael's interment ceremony, I got bits and pieces about how you and Mom brought him back. That wasn't enough for me. I need more backstory about you two. It's important to my origin story — and to Katya's, too."

"I'll take it for action."

"Good. And another suggestion. Have Katya do a TikTok or at least help you put a soundtrack to your podcast. She's a wizard at tech, and I know your musical tastes are a bit dated."

"Copy all, son. Trust me, the final product will have her finger-prints on it."

Charlie paced around the bench, gazing into the woods. I sensed my son was anxious. He turned and pointed to the drone. "Is Clarence recording now?"

"No. I turned him off. No one can see or hear us."

His pacing intensified. I took that as my cue to join him. "Do you know where they are sending you, Private?"

He took a deep breath. "The rumor is Afghanistan. It doesn't matter to me, though. I'll go wherever they send me. The Middle East, Asia, Europe, Africa, downtown Washington, D.C. There's plenty of hate going around and people who need our help. I just want to go where the fight is."

It was my turn for a deep breath. "My job now as a private citizen is to make sure you are fighting for the right reason." I put my arm around him. "We owe you that. *I* owe you that — and so much more."

Looking at my son, I felt the weight of decades of experience that separate us. I was a worn-out, retired Navy officer. He was the picture of youth—a lean, green Marine getting ready for his first operational assignment. How much advice did I offer him growing up, and how much did he absorb? Did I give him at least one tidbit of knowledge that would one day save his life? Launching my podcast had been inspired by Charlie's decision to serve in the armed forces. Over the next few weeks, I intended to tell him—and the world—stories that took a lifetime to unfold. My Navy career is abundant with plot lines, but I don't want to put myself at the center of any story. Like Razz's retelling of his rescue mission, I feel like my shipmates and comrades should feature as the most important characters.

The morning breeze calmed as we waited for the guests to arrive. After summoning Clarence, I watched the drone reposition to the tree line with Charlie. The cicadas were louder than before, their natural buzz easily overtaking the drone's stealthy hum. A cicada landed on my gold-starred shoulder board. Charlie reached to flick it off.

"Leave it, son," I said. "He's fine."

A shout came from the school's traffic circle. "Charlie!" Katya leaped out of our family car, burst through the playground gate, and sprinted up the hill. My joy was filled as this sweet jewel hugged her stepbrother with a smile brighter than the sun.

MICHAEL HAD BEEN CHARLIE'S AGE when he answered the call of duty in Vietnam. As teachers sit on the memorial bench, seeking relief from aching backs, worn knees, or classroom stress, I want them to consider the tragedy—and triumph—this young man experienced in a far-off land. As a son of this town and an alumnus of Woodland Hill Elementary School, he deserved it all.

As children explore the woods and walk the nature trail, I want them to feel as if they, too, are in a far-off land, yet a land no different from their home. The children may be too young for Michael's full story now, but therein lies the beauty of podcasting. Michael's story can live forever on the Internet, ready when they are.

I was not sure how to handle Charlie's grander request for a backstory about Lori and me. How do you communicate an unresolved love story against a backdrop of perpetual conflict and political chaos? Any attempt would barely disguise my certainty of the challenges Charlie will face in his own military career. Conflict and confusion always accompany the uniform. Even if he and his generation rise to meet the challenges left over from my generation, they will encounter new ones. Charlie and I are part of a cycle, one I'm leaving behind and he is just beginning.

As I waited atop the high ground for Lori to join me, I offered my palm to the cicada on my shoulder board. He, at least, broke free of his shell and took flight in search of love today.

Emergence Day offers an opportunity to contemplate where we are going. Memorial Day provides the time—and space—to think about where we have all been. This was our day to meet and honor a true hero. To renew bonds of friendship and to part ways in search of new adventures. To be with family, and who knows—it might even turn out to be a day to don the old catcher's gear and, at age sixty-two, see if these creaky old baseball knees can hold their own.

As Katya wandered the forest with Charlie, I walked past the bench adorned with a powder blue ribbon and ducked under a second ribbon strung across the start of the nature walk. The density of cicadas buzzing around the entrance was impressive—their chorus matched the frequency of my tinnitus, which had been sporadic over the years but was now a permanent nuisance.

A third, unexpected, yellow ribbon on a familiar black oak caught my eye. It was the same tree I had affixed with caution tape for Lori many years back. I hadn't put it there but it was elegant, and clearly meant for today. As I pondered the bow, I picked hollow cicada exoskeletons from the oak's bark. These ghost shells, cracked along their backsides and empty of their metamorphosed occupants, gripped tight to the tree bark as if still alive. It was one of the many wonders of nature that Myers students were missing during the pandemic lockdown.

I dialed Jason's number and his face popped onto my screen. "What's up, Admiral?"

"Are you ready to take over the drone?"

I heard a few keystrokes. "I have a positive data link."

"Today is a tough day for Leslie. Please keep Clarence away from her. I want to respect her privacy and not add to any awkwardness when Lori arrives."

"Copy that, boss."

I popped the drone control screen up on my phone and entered a code. "What's mine is now yours."

"I have command of Clarence," he said.

"Is Mom there?"

"She just walked in." The phone screen pivoted to her.

"Hi, Peter!"

"Love you, Mom. Thanks for skipping yoga this morning." She blew me a kiss. The phone screen pivoted back to Jason. "Do you have the drone locked on me? I'm walking out of the woods now."

As I approached the entrance of the forest, Clarence hovered above the trees, turning his camera toward me. Jason made him bounce up and down as if the drone were nodding his head. "Very cute, Clarence. I'll take that as a yes. Now go bother the kids."

I returned my eyes to my phone. "Jason, Patty and Stacey are coming out of the school. I need to go now. But do me a favor and test the loudspeaker. I need folks in the parking lot to be able to hear you."

The drone flew to a spot just over Katya and Charlie, who were fixated on its movements. "Hello-o-o, Patty! Hello-o-o, Stacey!" Jason's baritone voice burst over the cicada howls through the drone's speaker system. Patty and Stacey waved back.

Turning its camera to the youngsters below, the drone greeted them. "Hello, Katybug. Looking sharp, Charlie!"

"Hello, Uncle Jason," Katya answered.

"Cool toy, Uncle Jay," Charlie added.

"Hey, Katya, have you named the robot camper yet?"

"Yes!" she responded, whispering something to Charlie.

"I like it," Charlie said.

"Let's have it, doodle bug."

"Winnie Bagel," Katya replied, beaming.

"Love it!" said Jason. "I am officially done with naming things. You have the job now, Katya. Want to talk to Nana?"

My mother piped in. "Hello, Katya. Doesn't Charlie look so handsome? Charlie, give your mother a big hug from me. I know Lori is so proud of you, as we all are."

Charlie blushed. "Thank you, Nana. I will."

"Okay, team," I said. "Let's get this celebration going. We have guests coming up the ridge. Katya, will you greet Miss Patty and

Miss Stacey and escort them to Michael's bench? Charlie, your Papi and mother should be arriving soon. Best you get yourself to the roundabout and see if they need any assistance getting up this hill."

As my progenies went to their assigned duties and Clarence rose to his assigned altitude, I sent a text message to Leslie: "I love you."

Katya announced Stacey and Patty's arrival with a shout. "It's okay to hug everyone! No one has the virus."

"Thank you for the public health update, Katybug," I said, greeting Patty with a hug. "Happy birthday, dear friend."

"Oh, Peter! You have done so much for me and my family. This is overwhelming."

"Before you cry, Miss Patty, you have to cut the ribbon on Michael's bench." I nodded to Katya, who handed her a pair of scissors.

"Thank you, Katya."

Patty turned to the bench. "I hereby open this bench for sitting in the name of my beautiful brother, Michael." She cut the ribbon and invited Katya to sit with her. I waited till Stacey finished taking a picture and then gave her a hug, too.

"It's so good to see you again, Doctor."

"And in person! It's been too long, Peter. Technical meetings on the computer are fun, but there is no substitute for human contact."

"Agreed," I replied.

Stacey was referring to our weekly teleconferences—where we have laid the groundwork for our latest collaboration, a small business that applies advanced analytics to behavioral health. We are trying to merge Jason's algorithmic magic with her postdoctoral research on basic psychological needs, motivation, and wellness. The tech part is easy. Capturing the underpinnings of human behavior under stress is not.

My role in the company is more of "lab rat." Much like the system I designed for capturing veteran narratives about missing soldiers, our proposed wellness-monitoring system will mine real-time narrative from individuals—me, as a start—and compare it against known outcomes. With the goal of offering intervention at the earliest sign of departure from wellness, we envision building a robot battle buddy—someone you can talk to when human companionship is not available or is unreliable.

My contacts in the Department of Defense were very interested in a practical product that could mitigate battlefield stress. NASA wanted an algorithm for a manned Mars mission.

But my motivation was Charlie.

A honking horn alerted us to the arrival of a shiny van carrying Lori and her father, Patch. "Such a lovely sight," Patty said as Charlie lifted the frail soldier—decked out in his full United States Marine Corps dress blue uniform—and placed him into his iBot 5000, a state-of-the-art self-powered techno-wheelchair.

At the rear of the van, Leslie and Lori stood chatting. I grew anxious as I watched my wife laugh and embrace my life-long best friend—one the mother to my adopted daughter Katya—and the other the mother of my adopted son Charlie. I shifted awkwardly and looked up at Clarence hovering over the playground. I hoped that Jason was not filming the ladies.

Patch rolled through the playground gate to the bottom of the ridge with Charlie marching by his side. Lori trailed them, but Charlie dropped back to join her, leaving Patch to motor his wheelchair solo.

I shifted from concerned observer to proud compatriot as I watched Patch take the ridge, his iBot's gyro-stabilized wheels gripping the sloping terrain while the chair's seat auto-adjusted its angle to keep his body level.

My phone vibrated with a text from Jason. "Rolling Thunder arriving." I had known the motorcycles were coming, but a chill still went down my spine as I heard the roar of bikes blasting in formation. Many were affixed with POW-MIA flags, symbolizing advocacy for missing or forgotten soldiers of foreign wars. The leather-clad riders were from the Norfolk-based chapter of the national nonprofit Rolling Thunder. At my request, they had changed their annual morning ride through downtown D.C. to make a side trip in honor of Michael and his family.

On the lead bike rode retired Navy SEAL and Chief Petty Officer Moore and his new wife. "Old lady" is a term of endearment in the biker world, and Noy looked every bit the part as she dismounted with her husband, posting an American flag between them. It had been an honor to preside over their wedding and administer the oath of allegiance to Noy as she became a naturalized citizen. Not all patriots are homegrown.

A fifty-bike squadron flanked the two, idling their engines as Patch finished the technology-assisted climb up the ridge to my position. His right arm, thin and shaking, raised his boney fingers to his cover in a salute. I returned the honor, and together we pivoted toward Moore, Noy, and the ensign.

As Clarence blared the national anthem, I stole a peripheral view. Patty and Lori were in front of the bench with their hands over their hearts. Charlie, next to Lori, was a statue of honor while Katya sang every word loud and proud under the howl of bugs and the reverberation of the music off the water tower on the distant hill. Stacey, standing behind Patty, was a wet mess of tears.

As the anthem finished, I looked past Moore and Noy to Leslie, who was standing hand over heart outside of Winnie Bagel. On the final note, the motorcycle squadron revved in unison, creating a roar that rattled windows in the housing development next door.

Patch and I turned to face each other once more. Charlie, acting as my adjutant, handed me the Silver Star citation folder. He stood by my side and held the medallion casing open for Patch to see. Moore had commanded the brigade to shut down their bikes, dismount, and stand at attention. Meanwhile, Jason positioned Clarence over my shoulder to record and blare my words to the bikers in the parking lot.

I read the medal citation, which in three sentences summarized events that we can never prove happened exactly as stated. But the words served their purpose. The boilerplate closing, after all, is what matters most. "His actions reflect the highest credit upon himself and the United States Army. He gallantly gave his life in the service of his country." Charlie pinned the medal on Patch's uniform above his Purple Heart ribbon that was adorned with four oak-leaf clusters.

I stood to the side to let the older man absorb the moment. He pivoted his robot chair to face the bikers in the parking lot. With Charlie's assistance, he gingerly rose from the chair and stood on his own two feet. The bikers cheered and waved flags. Patch whispered to Charlie in a broken, cracked voice, "He's home, Charlie. Michael is home. He always finds his way back."

I motioned to Patty and Lori, who came forward and embraced their father. Katya and Stacey joined me and we eased ourselves backward out of the limelight. Cicadas swirled around Patch and his family as they poured out pent-up emotions upon each other. Patch trembled with fatigue, so Charlie carried him to the bench, where he sat at peace.

My phone vibrated. "Got to roll, Admiral," said Moore. "Thank you for letting us be part of this honor."

"Perfectly executed, Chief," I replied. "Godspeed to you and your bride. But don't go quite yet." I walked to Lori and handed her my phone. "There's a couple of bikers who want to say hi to you."

Lori, still shaking with emotion, cried into the phone, "I love you guys. Thank you so much. Noy, call me later. Chief, you are the best. Hugs to all your club for me."

I was close enough to hear Noy's reply to Lori as she shouted over the roaring engines. "Congratulations, Madam Ambassador."

Together Lori and I waved as Noy and Chief rode the backdoor of the formation out of the school parking lot, taking most of the noise with them. Then I turned to her, eyes wide. "Ambassador?"

She grabbed my arm and put a finger to her lips. "Shhh. It's not public yet, and I haven't told Charlie." She turned toward her family to see if anyone else had heard the phone conversation over the chorus of cicadas and the rumble of motorcycles. They hadn't, so she added in a half-whisper, "I'm being elevated by the State Department, but it's not official until the White House signs off."

"They will," I said, smiling.

"They started the vetting process. There's a ton of paperwork." Her excitement came down a notch.

"No doubt," I said as I led her away from the bench.

"And then there will be Senate committee hearings."

"No sweat. You've been there before."

"And a floor vote."

"Not a problem."

"Did I mention host-country approval?"

"Which country?"

"To be determined. Likely the East Asia and Pacific bureau, though."

"You sound hesitant," I said. "Like you don't want the job…"

She gave no immediate response. We stared back at the bench. Charlie and Patch were laughing, sharing military tales. Katya and Stacey both had cicadas in their hands, and Patty was reading Michael's citation.

"I *do* want the job," she finally said.

"I know you do. Come on. There's another ribbon to cut for the new nature walk."

Charlie helped Patch back into his iBot5000, and Lori locked arms with Patty and Stacey to lead them to the next ribbon. Patch was handed the scissors but balked at the honor. "Where is my little Sputnik, Katya?"

Katya stepped forward. "Here I am."

Lori and Patty reacted in unison. "No eyeball tricks, Daddy."

He shooed his daughters with his hand and addressed Katya. "Young lady? The woods are a classroom," he said. "Will you do me the honor of opening up the forest for the children of this school?"

My sweet daughter proudly cut the ribbon to the cheers of the adults. Then she, Charlie, and Patch led our procession down the fresh wood-chip path lined with ferns and an assortment of flowering plants. Just off the path, woody vines twisted around towering elms and oaks, as squirrels darted across limbs that stretched over the trail. Afternoon sunlight penetrated the canopy, creating a checkered pattern of light and shadow on the trees and brush, illuminating the way for an eleven-year old's sense of adventure and a teacher's sense of security.

Stacey and Patty, holding hands, followed behind Patch's chair. Lori retrieved the scissors from Charlie and took my arm. We dropped back until the voices of the humans disappeared into the forest. We were alone with the cicadas.

"This looks a lot like the forest in Laos," she said.

"The trees are smaller. And there are no tigers,…that I know of."

We walked to the eastern black oak that was adorned with the yellow ribbon. Lori, silent as we approached it, handed me the pair of scissors. "Are we cutting this ribbon too?" I asked.

"Yes, we are," she replied, squeezing my hand.

"Should we wait for the others? The ribbon's for Michael."

She looked at me. "Is it, though?" She plucked a cicada shell from the oak and placed it on my uniform. "Why did you put the original ribbon here, Peter? You know…the yellow construction tape from the ball field?"

"It was a promise to you. It would remain until Michael came home."

She nodded. "Yes, *you* made that promise, Peter, and you kept it. So this ribbon is for you. You are free."

I looked down the path. The entourage was not in sight. I knew Clarence was in a hold pattern outside of the woods. I was alone with

Lori and the Brood X inhabitants of Woodland Hill. I cut the ribbon, turned, and handed it to her. The mission was accomplished and the cycle had ended.

Not every moment can be explained, but in that one, something shifted. Suddenly, I was riding the emotional rescue hoist up again, trying my best to hold on to someone—or something—valuable and precious. The ride itself was short and would end but, in that moment, I was in between. I was past the beginning but not yet at the finale, experiencing the bliss that I had often felt—playing in a ballgame, flying an aircraft, or simply being with my family.

The moment ended with the return of the entourage. Lori and I rejoined the group, and together we exited the woods and went back to the bench and an open sky full of cicadas. We said our initial goodbyes, and I "retired" Patty with the traditional Navy send-off: "Fair winds and following seas." The ceremony was over, but I suddenly realized I had no idea of how to transition to a graceful ending.

Hugs, kisses, embraces, and salutes. All were exchanged for the first time since Michael's interment at Arlington. The pandemic had made everyone forget the power and comfort of human touch. For me, it was a welcome return from isolation to unapologetic humanity.

Stacey, the intellect of the bunch, recognized what needed to come next and signaled to me. "Let's give the family a moment alone."

I nodded. "Good call, Professor." I waved Katya over and asked her if she would push Stacey on the playground swing set in exchange for Winnie Bagel driving time on the way to Beavercreek, Ohio—our first stop on the trip west.

While Katya and Stacey went off toward the swings, I took a direct path to the baseball field for one last squat behind home plate. I twisted my Navy cap backward and imagined catching a hanging curve ball as it bounced in front of home plate. I heard the distant echo of an authoritative shout of "strike three" from an umpire who appreciated a well-called pitch from a gritty, conniving, and determined baseball catcher.

My imaginary pitcher was soon replaced on the mound by Clarence. Jason was still piloting from his office in California. I pulled out my phone and called him. "Mom isn't watching, is she?"

"No, she's not. Chez stopped by to watch the ceremony and pay her respects. They stepped out for coffee while you guys were bird watching or whatever you were doing in the woods."

"Please give Chez my best wishes. None of this would have been possible without her help. And yours."

"Not needed," Jason replied. He sent Clarence to perform an airshow, choreographed to his own unique interpretation of patriotic music. The show caught the attention of the playground pair and the four residents of Michael's bench.

"Are you ready for the big finish?" he said. "We need to end this episode so we can all move on."

"Give me a minute," I said. "I'm getting a different vibe and need to adjust the gouge. I'll text you when I'm ready." I hung up and gazed at my surroundings. Katya was still swinging with Auntie Stacey. I turned my attention to the bench, where Lori and Charlie sat in the middle seats. Patty sat to Charlie's left as they softly chatted. Lori, meanwhile, had locked tight onto her father's arm, her head resting on his shoulder. I knew that face — it was a face of contentment.

I texted Jason. "Ready when you are." ·

Clarence returned to the mound and pointed his camera at me. I dipped my head to remove my hat and dusted a thin sheen of dirt from my white uniform trousers. Remembering the ghost shell of the cicada that Lori had placed on my shoulder, I plucked it off and held it in my fingers.

17

Gouge: Episode 1

Good afternoon, shipmates, and welcome to Gouge. I'm your podcast host, Admiral Pete. Thank you for joining this live stream special Memorial Day event. I am standing on the ball field of Michelle Myers Charter School, located among the horse farms and wineries surrounding the northern Virginia town of Woodland Hill. Myers Charter holds a special place in my heart. This is where I "got the gouge" that would shape me in my youth, sustain me throughout my career, and fulfill me in retirement. This podcast is my way of passing gouge on to you.

I have a new mission in life. I love stories of perseverance and resilience. These are the stories I want to share with you. The goal is to motivate and help you navigate the turbulent seas of life you might be encountering.

I've collected these stories from shipmates and colleagues over my thirty-five years as a naval officer and from post-retirement friends who share my passion for community service. The heroes of my stories are everyday people who work hard, build team unity, and have a knack for fun. Work hard, be nice, and have fun – simple gouge to get you through any challenge.

A shout-out to my brother, Jason, for letting me borrow Clarence to record this event. Clarence is a drone named to honor the guardian angel from the classic movie It's a Wonderful Life. *Jason deserves all credit for* the video production of these live streams. He is one of the many guardian angels I count on to get me through my personal challenges. He controls Clarence from his office in Silicon Valley, California. Any crash, collision, or air space violation is on him. If all goes well, I will take the full credit.

We bundled a few ribbon cutting events in this episode. The Myers Charter Foundation recently purchased the swath of property behind the new memorial bench on the ridge. The bench rests at the entrance to a nature walk carved out of the woods with help from local veterans. Myers students now have access to life science wonders in their own backyard – of course, once pandemic restrictions are lifted. We also honored Principal Patty for her many years of service to education.

But the true purpose of today's gathering was the high military honor bestowed on Patty's brother, Michael, awarded posthumously to his father, Patch – a disabled veteran of the Korean War, ninety-eight years young. Michael served in the Vietnam War and died in combat – a tragic story. But in life, tragedy and triumph somehow coexist. Triumph is hard to find in the fog of tragedy, but I know many resilient military families who do. Their stories inspire me. In future episodes, I plan to share them with you.

There is no mistaking the buzz of Brood X male cicadas in the background. I'm holding the ghost shell of one in my hand. Magicicada septendecim have survived seventeen years burrowed in solitude – and are now molted for the last time. In their final stage of development, they are flying around the school playground, searching for true love. Their life cycle puts a time stamp on our own developmental transitions. I am sixty-two years old, and this is my fourth emergence cycle. With each one, I have learned new life lessons and have hopefully grown as a person. Seventeen years from now, I hope to emerge totally enlightened. Let's set that as a goal to achieve together.

Meanwhile, the bug who once inhabited this shell is now a novice aviator flying high above and looking down at the ground, much like Clarence. He has a view of a world still at war. Little has changed over the seventeen years since he popped out of his egg and burrowed through the dirt. Soldiers continue soldiering. Humans still use conflict to resolve conflict. From a macro-distant perspective, we seem to know little of who we are and how to organize to achieve common goals that lead to peace and prosperity for all.

But…if he flew low enough, our aviating bug learned about Michael and each person connected by his story. There is sadness and enduring pain in each of us — we all experience lasting regret when those whom we love are no longer physically here.

But each is alive in our hearts. They live in our minds as narratives, the stories we create for and about them. Narratives give good gouge and remind us not to take on the world alone. We can solve problems as a team and meet challenges together. Michael taught us that.

Days like today — Memorial Day for humans and Emergence Day for the cicadas — serve a clarifying purpose. Today, we appreciate the wings we have been given. These wings help us rise above sadness, regroup our thoughts, reset our lives, and fly again to start another cycle.

May we happily look for teammates with whom to share the journey, and vow to help the lost bugs we encounter along the way.

I stared straight into Clarence's camera eye and announced to Jason, "That's a wrap."

"I'm on it," he said. "I got great aerial shots of the whole area — the bench, the ceremony, the school, the trail — to edit in. You're gonna love it."

I pulled my phone out of my back pocket and punched in the code to retake drone control. I let out a deep breath as Clarence landed and shut down. Katya ran over. "Here. Hold this for me." She dropped a marble in my hand.

"Where did you get this?" I asked, trying not to laugh, though I recognized it by its eyeball size and ivory color.

"Papi gave it to me. He said it was for good luck on our trip."

I hoisted Clarence over my shoulder and gave the marble back to Katya.

"Are you ready for our next adventure, Katybug?"

"Yup," she replied. I took her hand and we walked to the parking lot and the RV.

Leslie helped me stow Clarence into his container. When I turned to look at her, the hair stood up on the back of my neck. The answer for how we'd move on was suddenly clear.

I had clung to Lori's hand since that night at the skating rink long before, and she had finally let go. It would take some time to get used to, but I was free now—as Lori said—to love my wife with all my heart.

Katya tugged on my sleeve. "Can I drive first?"

"Of course you can," I said. And then I removed my cap and raced her to the door.

EPILOGUE

The Bliss of the In-Between

Aviation magic lifts me up to the sky.
I point the nose upward and set the altitude high;
At maximum thrust, my contrails are seen,
As I soar through the bliss of the in-between.

I look to the stars at the onset of night,
Awed by their beauty—such a heavenly sight—
The universe is large, so vast and clean,
Imparting its joy to the in-between.

On top of the clouds, I look down below
And view a perspective the hawks only know;
Conflict and strife are but a constant routine
When viewed from the bliss of the in-between.

The sight is chilling, as the people I see
Are fighting and crying and calling to me.
What I wouldn't give to reverse such a scene
To hear joy fill the void of the in-between.

To ailing brethren, all comfort and aid
Must be tirelessly spent and selflessly paid.
A force united must be heard and be seen
Injecting hope and love to the in-between.

If earthbound I stay for the rest of my life,
Let me yearn for the stars, far from all strife;
The sky is my dream—my heart beats its wings
To thrive in the bliss of the in-between.

The mission to account for and repatriate US personnel displaced by conflict and war continues. For current information on these efforts, contact the Defense POW/MIA Accounting Agency.

https://www.dpaa.mil

Let us never forget.

About the Author

KEN RYAN LIVES IN MOUNT Pleasant, South Carolina, where he founded a small business for innovative research and creative writing following a thirty-year career in the US Navy. This novel, his first, is reflective of his time in uniform. Fiction is his chosen vehicle to communicate a message of hope to readers who may be overwhelmed by headlines and uninformed about the US military and its inner workings.

www.ingramcontent.com/pod-product-compliance
Lightning Source LLC
Chambersburg PA
CBHW042315120626

46547CB00022B/2105